Gradient
Knits

Copyright © 2017 Quarto Publishing plc

First edition for North America published in 2017 by
Barron's Educational Series, Inc.

All inquiries should be addressed to:
Barron's Educational Series, Inc.
250 Wireless Boulevard
Hauppauge, New York 11788
www.barronseduc.com

ISBN: 978-1-4380-1059-5

Library of Congress Control Number: 2017936679

QUMMSKN

This book was conceived, designed, and produced by:
Quantum Books Ltd, an imprint of The Quarto Group
6 Blundell Street
London N7 9BH
United Kingdom

Publisher: Kerry Enzor
Editorial: Julia Shone and Emma Harverson
Evaluator: Jodi Lewanda
Technical Consultant: Therese Chynoweth
Designer: Rosamund Saunders
Photographers: Simon Pask and Brandy Crist-Travers
Production Manager: Rohana Yusof

Printed in China by 1010 Printing International Ltd

9 8 7 6 5 4 3 2 1

Tanis Gray

Gradient
Knits

10 lessons and projects using ombré, stranded colorwork, slip-stitch, and texture

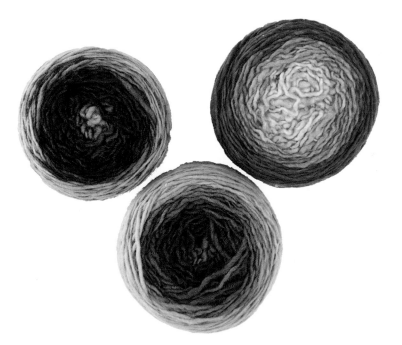

Contents

Chapter 2: Lessons & Projects   16

Introduction

What makes us gravitate toward gradient yarns?
Personally, I've always found choosing the right color for
my knits to be like embarking on an exciting quest.

Knitters are spoiled today with color options coming at us from all sides, from commercially dyed options to the stunning spectrum supplied by talented hand dyers. Gradients add an extra layer of interest to our knitting, allowing us to use myriad colors without additional work. Why cast on with a solid color when you can knit with a batch of mini skeins or with a rainbow cascading from one skein?

I learned to knit when I was eight years old and have always felt drawn toward the bright yarns on the shelf. My mind was blown when I was introduced to stranded colorwork knitting and I was suddenly able to combine my adoration of color and love of knitting into a single project. To this day I am a Fair Isle addict and often look for ways to sneak more colors into my knitting. Gradients are an excellent way to do this, and I find myself reaching for them regularly.

As a knitwear designer and knitting instructor, spreading the word about knitting and the amazing things that can be accomplished with sticks and yarn brings me great joy. Knitting delivers wonderful health benefits, and we can change our outlook using the psychology of color in the fibers and hues that we work with.

While gradients and gradient sets have been on the market for years, they have recently become even more widely available to us at fiber festivals and local yarn stores across the globe. When teaching, I often hear, "I love gradients, but I just don't know what to do with them." If you feel that way, then this book will be your guide, and will get you exploring techniques and gradient options again and again. I hope you come to feel as passionately about color as I do!

Tania

How to Use This Book

Gradients are a perfect way to add a unique dimension to your knitting. Go from light to dark, use two-color contrasts, or work with multiple colorways—the possibilities are endless!

The ten simple lessons in this book will take you from your first knitting stitch through to more advanced colorwork—giving you all of the skills you need to incorporate gradients successfully into your knitting. Each lesson includes a brief introduction to the technique, followed by clear, step-by-step photography that takes you through stitch by stitch, and then finishes with a beautiful project to put your newfound skills to the test. The projects have

been specially designed for this book by a range of fantastic knitwear designers—find out more about them on pages 135–137.

The lessons build on one another as you move through the book, so start at the beginning and work from Lesson 1 to Lesson 10 for a full introduction to knitting with gradients.

Each new lesson starts with an introduction to what you will learn on the following pages.

Step-by-step photographs take you through each new knitting skill.

Any materials needed to complete the project are listed in the "You Will Need" panel at the beginning of each project. The type of yarn is specified for each project along with the suggested colors. See pages 138–139 for a comprehensive list of yarns used in the book.

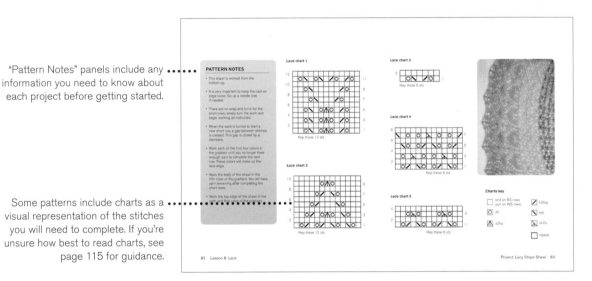

project: COLOR-STUDY COWL

Using slip-stitch is an excellent way to dip your toes into colorwork knitting. This chic bandana-shaped cowl makes use of the darkest color in the gradient, which is slip-stitched against a stockinette background using the lighter colors. Beginning with a traditional garter tab cast-on typically seen in shawl construction, the sport-weight cowl is worked flat, back and forth, and increased at the center and edges. Once the cowl has reached the optimal width, the work is joined in the round and finished with a classic i-cord bind off. Complete the look by adding a gradient fringe along the bottom front.

YOU WILL NEED
• Yarn Weight: Sport
• Blend: 100% Superwash Merino
• Yardage: 60 yd. (54 m) skeins
• Colors: 6 colors, C1–C6 (darkest to lightest)
• Needle: US size 5 (3.75 mm) circular needle (or size needed to obtain gauge), 20 in. (50 cm) long
• Tapestry needle
• 3 stitch markers

Gauge: 24 sts and 34 rows = 4 in. (10 cm) in blocked stockinette stitch.

Approximate Finished Size:
Neck opening: 22 in. (56 cm);
Center-front: 15 in. (38 cm);
Center-back: 5¾ in. (17 cm)

26   Lesson 2: Slip-Stitch

"Pattern Notes" panels include any information you need to know about each project before getting started.

Some patterns include charts as a visual representation of the stitches you will need to complete. If you're unsure how best to read charts, see page 115 for guidance.

PATTERN NOTES
• This shawl is worked from the bottom up.
• It is very important to keep the cast-on edge loose. Go up a needle size if needed.
• There are no wrap and turns for the short rows; simply turn the work and begin working as instructed.
• When the work is turned to start a new short row, a gap between stitches is created. This gap is closed by a decrease.
• Work each of the first four colors in the gradient until you no longer have enough yarn to complete the next row. These colors will make up the lace edge.
• Work the body of the shawl in the fifth color of the gradient. You will have yarn remaining after completing the short rows.
• Work the top edge of the shawl in the sixth (or final) color of the gradient.

Lace chart 1

Lace chart 3

Lace chart 4

Lace chart 2

Lace chart 5

Charts key
☐ knit on RS rows / purl on WS rows
○ yo
◢ s2kp
╱ k2tog
╲ ssk
⬛ sk2p
☐ repeat

82   Lesson 8: Lace

Project: Lacy Stripe Shawl   83

Before beginning a project, check out the Basic Knitting Techniques chapter, pages 106–134, for all the techniques you need to get started—from measuring gauge to casting on—and a full list of knitting stitch abbreviations.

Step-by-step photographs clearly show how to complete each skill.

Circular Knitting

When working on a project that is circular, such as a hat, pair of gloves or socks, or a cowl, knitting in the round is an obvious choice. For these items, circular knitting results in much faster knitting, with a more even gauge, and the finished item fits better than if the work were knit flat and seamed.

USING CIRCULAR NEEDLES

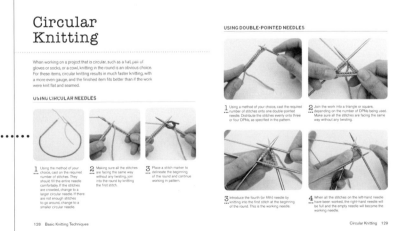

1 Using the method of your choice, cast on the required number of stitches. They should fit the entire needle comfortably. If the stitches are crowded, change to a larger circular needle. If there are not enough stitches to go around, change to a smaller circular needle.

2 Making sure all the stitches are facing the same way without any twisting, join into the round by knitting the first stitch.

3 Place a stitch marker to delineate the beginning of the round and continue working in pattern.

USING DOUBLE-POINTED NEEDLES

1 Using a method of your choice, cast the required number of stitches onto one double-pointed needle. Distribute the stitches evenly onto three or four DPNs as specified in the pattern.

2 Join the work into a triangle or square, depending on the number of DPNs being used. Make sure all the stitches are facing the same way without any twisting.

3 Introduce the fourth (or fifth) needle by knitting into the first stitch at the beginning of the round. This is the working needle.

4 When all the stitches on the left-hand needle have been worked, the right-hand needle will be full and the empty needle will become the working needle.

128   Basic Knitting Techniques

Circular Knitting   129

CHAPTER 1
Choosing the Right Gradient

Unlock the mystery of gradient color. Here, you'll find tips on understanding color theory and how to apply this knowledge when choosing the perfect yarns for a gradient project.

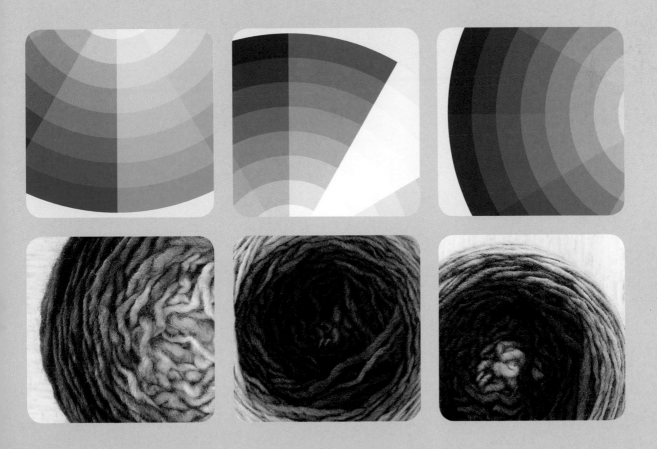

Basic Color Theory

Color can be tricky when it comes to knitting. You want to be sure your color choices don't turn muddy when you knit them together; you want them to show off your hard work and enhance the stitches, and you want a color combination that is enjoyable to knit.

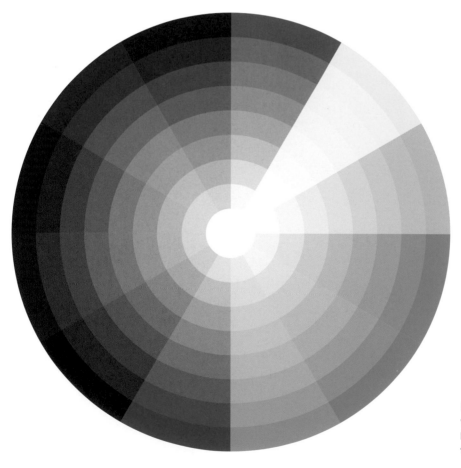

It is helpful to look at a color wheel to remind yourself how colors are arranged on the spectrum.

Sometimes, what you envisage working as a finished object, or what you see under good lighting in your local yarn store, looks completely different once you've worked a few rows at home. This can be both frustrating and disappointing, sending you right back to the drawing board.

Enter the gradients! Although they've been around for years, gradients have recently gained popularity in the yarn market. Gradient yarns remove the mystery of color combinations from the equation, offering up stunning light-to-dark ombré effects, or even color groupings that play off each other, which you may never have pulled together yourself.

THE COLOR WHEEL

There are five "main" colors—black, white, red, yellow, and blue—that are referred to as hues. The three colors that cannot be made from any other colors are red, blue, and yellow. These are called the primary colors, and they create a basis for the entire color wheel. You will see that they are evenly spaced out within the wheel and relate to one another. Put red and blue together to get purple; put yellow and blue together to create green; mix together red and yellow to get orange. These are called the secondary colors, and if they are split around the wheel again, we get yellow-orange, red-orange, red-purple, etc. These are tertiary colors, made by mixing a primary and a secondary together.

So, how does the color wheel help us with knitting? It comes down to aesthetics and using color theory to help us put together combinations that work well together, which is sometimes referred to as color harmony. Colors have relationships with one another—if it's a good match, your knitting will sing! A good color combination creates the same kind of

harmony for your eyes that a well-written piece of music will for your ears.

Generally speaking, colors that live across from one another on the wheel work well together; these are called complementary colors. It's also possible to add in a third color, evenly spaced between the two complementary colors on the wheel, to create split complementaries.

Analogous colors—groups of three to four colors that are situated side by side on the wheel—also work well together.

TINTS, SHADES, AND TONE

Black and white do not appear on the color wheel but are very powerful, so don't shy away from them. Black and white are used to create tints and shades of the colors that appear on the wheel when mixed in. The tint is manipulated when white is added to a color—think of the colors you often see in the baby yarn section of a knitting store. The shade is manipulated by adding in black—this is seen a lot in fall and winter yarns, or what some people refer to as "manly shades." If you add both black and white to a hue, you are manipulating the tone. This tones down the saturation of the original hues on the wheel, and they look slightly grayed out.

You certainly don't have to work in the same tone, shade, or tint when you're creating your color schemes for gradient knitting, but if your combination doesn't feel quite right, look at the yarn and see if it has black, white, or both added in and re-evaluate your choice.

Gradient Options

Gradient yarn sets come in many incarnations, from ombré sets to single-skein gradients. The following is a guide to the different types, how to choose which to use, and how to use them. Once you have the perfect gradient yarns in your hands, you are ready to cast on and create beautiful gradient knits.

OMBRÉ SETS

Ombré gradient sets feature one color changing gradually from pale to dark. While ombré sets often come in fingering-weight yarn, many larger companies and independent dyers are offering up more weights to choose from. The Gradient Block Cowl on page 51 is a great example of using this type of yarn.

COLOR GROUPINGS

Other gradient sets supply color combinations that include completely different hues, encouraging the knitter to step out of their comfort zone. The Festoon Mittens on page 60 make use of an interesting color blend that works together in such harmony that it's like a perfectly composed song.

Ombré sets allow you to gradually change one color from light to dark.

SINGLE-SKEIN GRADIENT YARNS

Another option is using single-skein gradients, many of which offer enough yardage to produce an entire small project. Single-skein gradient yarns come in both short and long striping patterns, or go through the entire rainbow without any repeat colors. Short striping skeins are ideal for projects like socks or fingerless mitts. Due to the frequent change in color, short striping gradients tend to look better with simple stitch work, letting the color be the star. For example, in the Blocket Hat design on page 21, a simple stitch pattern allows the stunning yarn to do a lot of work for the knitter.

With longer color repeats (and, in some cases, no repeat colors at all), the colors featured will often dictate whether to go for a simple or complex stitch pattern, and projects with more complicated stitch work will be shown off to their advantage. Gradient yarn comes in so many wonderful colorways, it's difficult to choose just one. The Zigzag Legwarmers on page 71 show that each color gets only one chance in the spotlight, making the eyes feast upon each color individually.

CREATE YOUR OWN GRADIENT SET

Of course, you could gather your own gradient set. Grab your color wheel and head to your local yarn store with an idea in mind—do you want to go ombré or try your hand at a color grouping? With yarn companies adding more and more shades to their palettes, it's easy to make a custom gradient set and get exactly what you want. Don't forget that neutrals are colors too and can make an alluring gradient set.

If you feel like donning your "mad scientist" hat, there are also informative online tutorials on how

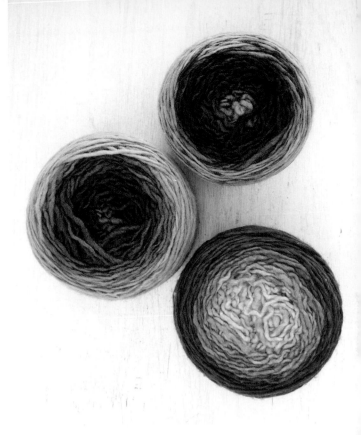

With single-skein gradient yarns, you can work gradients into your knitting without changing yarns.

to dye your own gradient yarns, many using simple food dyes and chemical-free ingredients. What a fantastic way to make a custom yarn for yourself or a knitting friend!

NOW, GET KNITTING

What happens after you have the perfect gradient yarns in your hands and you are ready to cast on? Here's the good news—the sky is the limit when knitting with gradients, and often it's the perfect chance to let the yarn do the talking. Color and stitch pattern in tandem can vie for attention, so simple stripes, basic chevron patterns, a classic knit and purl combination, lazy cables, or even a small lace repeat will show off colors to their benefit. The more variation in colors, the less complex the stitch pattern should be. Never be afraid to experiment.

CHAPTER 2
Lessons & Projects

The following ten lessons will teach you how to knit confidently with gradient yarns. Choose from knits and purls, slip-stitch, and cabling, or work your way through each technique before casting on for your project.

Lesson 1: Knit & Purl

Knit and purl stitches are the foundation of all knitted projects. Knitters can combine knits and purls to form a repeated pattern or construct a random sequence, rearrange them to form cables, increase and decrease with yarn overs to create lace, or work them in multiple colors for colorwork. Without knit and purl stitches, knitters would not be able to create unique techniques.

Requiring little more than yarn and needles, knitting was ideal for nomads who carried everything on their backs. They often traveled with animals that provided fiber to be spun and turned into yarn, ultimately becoming clothing and blankets.

The word "knitting" is thought to come from *knutten*, a Dutch verb meaning "to knot." The craft itself is thought to have originated in the Middle East and then spread via trading routes. Archeologists have found knitting in Egyptian tombs dating as far back as the eleventh century; other crafts, such as crochet, nalebinding, and sewing, have been found in similar archeological digs. It is unclear which technique came first, but all are said to have evolved from one another.

1 To make a knit stitch, with the yarn at the back, insert the right-hand needle into the stitch on the left-hand needle from front to back, making an "x" with the needles.

2 Wrap the yarn around the back of the right-hand needle counterclockwise.

3 Pull the right-hand needle down and to the front through the opening and slide the stitch off the left-hand needle, transferring it to the right-hand needle. This is a fully executed knit stitch.

4 To make a purl stitch, bring the yarn between
the needles to the front of the work.

5 Insert the right-hand needle into the front of
the stitch on the left-hand needle, making
an "x" with the needles. Wrap the yarn
around the front of the right-hand needle
counterclockwise.

6 Pull the right-hand
needle down and to
the back through the
opening and slide the
stitch off the left-hand
needle, transferring
it to the right-hand
needle. This is a fully
executed purl stitch.

project: BLOCKET HAT

A simple pattern of knits and purls paired with a striking gradient yarn can create a most elegant combination. Worked in the round from the bottom up, a textured pattern emerges that is enhanced by the gentle color changes of the worsted-weight gradient yarn. The ideal project for the knitter who is ready to move beyond scarves and try something more challenging, this unisex hat is knit in the round on a circular needle and culminates with crown decreases on double-pointed needles. This project will boost confidence, generate an interesting texture, and look sophisticated on everyone. Top it off with an optional pom-pom for a jaunty finish.

YOU WILL NEED

- **Yarn Weight: Worsted**
- **Blend: 100% merino wool**
- **Yardage: 284 yd. (260 m), 3½ oz. (100 g)**
- **Colors: 1 ball gradient yarn**
- **Needles: US size 5 (3.75 mm) circular needle, 16 in. (40 cm) long; US size 6 (4 mm) circular needle, 16 in. (40 cm) long; US size 6 (4 mm) double-pointed needles (DPNs) (or size needed to obtain gauge)**
- **Stitch marker**
- **Tapestry needle**

Gauge: 17 sts and 38 rounds = 4 in. (10 cm) in textured block pattern on larger circular needles

Approximate Finished Size: One size fits most adults, 22 in. (56 cm) brim circumference and 7½ in. (19 cm) high, including brim

TEXTURED BLOCK PATTERN

Rounds 1 and 10: [P1, k1] to end of round.

Round 2: [P2, (k1, p1) three times, k2] to end of round.

Round 3: [P3, (k1, p1) twice, k3] to end of round.

Round 4: [P4, k1, p1, k4] to end of round.

Rounds 5 and 6: [P5, k5] to end of round.

Round 7: [K1, p4, k4, p1] to end of round.

Round 8: [P1, k1, p3, k3, p1, k1] to end of round.

Round 9: [K1, p1, k1, p2, k2, p1, k1, p1] to end of round.

Rounds 11 and 20: [K1, p1] to end of round.

Round 12: [P1, k1, p1, k2, p2, k1, p1, k1] to end of round.

Round 13: [K1, p1, k3, p3, k1, p1] to end of round.

Round 14: [P1, k4, p4, k1] to end of round.

Rounds 15 and 16: [K5, p5] to end of round.

Round 17: [K4, p1, k1, p4] to end of round.

Round 18: [K3, (p1, k1) twice, p3] to end of round.

Round 19: [K2, (p1, k1) three times, p2] to end of round.

Repeat rounds 1–20 for pattern.

Chart for textured block pattern

●		●		●		●		●		20
●	●		●		●		●			19
●	●	●		●		●				18
●	●	●	●		●					17
●	●	●	●	●						16
●	●	●	●	●						15
	●	●	●	●					●	14
●		●	●	●				●		13
	●		●	●			●		●	12
●		●		●		●		●		11
	●		●		●		●		●	10
●		●		●	●		●			9
	●			●	●	●			●	8
●			●	●	●	●				7
		●	●	●	●	●				6
		●	●	●	●	●				5
			●		●	●	●	●		4
		●		●		●	●	●		3
	●		●		●		●	●		2
	●		●		●			●		1

Rep these 10 sts

Chart key

	knit
●	purl

TO MAKE THE HAT

Using the smaller circular needles, CO 100 sts using German Twisted CO method (see page 119). Join into round, taking care not to twist, pm for beginning of round.

Work in p1, k1tbl rib for 12 rounds.

With larger circular needles, begin the textured block pattern (see page 22 or chart, left), working rounds 1–20 three times, then rounds 1–3 once more.

Begin crown decreases, switching to DPNs when necessary.

Round 1: [(P2tog) twice, k1, p1, (k2tog) twice] to end of round. (60 sts)

Round 2: [P3, k3] to end of round.

Round 3: [P2tog, p1, k1, k2tog] to end of round. (40 sts)

Round 4: [P2, k2] to end of round.

Round 5: [P2tog, k2tog] to end of round. (20 sts)

Round 6: [P1, k1] to end of round.

Round 7: [K2tog] to end of round. (10 sts)

Round 8: [K2tog] to end of round. (5 sts)

FINISHING

Break yarn, weaving tail through remaining sts. Pull tight to close, secure on WS. Weave in all loose ends with tapestry needle. Block lightly. Make a 4 in. (10 cm) pom-pom (see panel opposite) and secure on center-top.

MAKING A POM-POM

- You can create a pom-pom easily using two circles of cardboard. Cut two circles out of cardboard, slightly larger than you want your finished pom-pom to be.

- In both circles, clip a small opening in the edge and cut a circle out of the middle. The hole in the middle should be slightly smaller than half the diameter of the outer circle.

- Place the cardboard circles together, with the openings lined up.

- Wind the yarn around and around the cardboard "donut," wrapping as evenly as possible.

- Keep wrapping until the center circle is nearly full.

- Using scissors, cut the outside edge of the wrapped yarn. Your scissors will be able to slide between the cardboard disks.

- Tie a string around the cut yarn by sliding it between the disks.

- Knot the string firmly, leaving long tails you can use for attaching the pom-pom.

- Trim the pom-pom to a spherical shape.

- Attach the pom-pom to your piece using the long tails.

Lesson 2: Slip-Stitch

Considered the easiest of the three main types of colorwork, the slip-stitch technique—often referred to as "mosaic knitting," a term coined by Barbara Walker in the 1960s—is an excellent introduction to colorwork in knitting.

Worked either in stockinette or garter stitch, multiple colors may be used, but only one color at a time is worked across a row or round, leaving the others behind. This makes the knitting much easier to manage. While some stitches are worked regularly, others are only slipped, with the yarn being held either to the front or back, generating elongated stitches in the previous color.

Simple to work both back and forth or in the round (as shown in the step sequence opposite), slip-stitch colorwork provides instant gratification because there is no need to juggle multiple bobbins, as for intarsia, and no need to carry multiple strands of yarn across the back of the work, as is done for Fair Isle. The end result is often a geometric, angular look with a thicker, somewhat stretchy fabric that works well for all types of accessories and garments.

1 Begin by slipping two stitches purlwise from
the left-hand needle to the right-hand needle.
The slipped stitches are in the old color
because they are slipped and not worked.

2 Introduce the new color and then knit
four stitches.

3 Continue in pattern to end of round.

4 Continue in pattern as written. The slipped
stitches will become elongated while the
stitches that are knitted remain standard,
creating the illusion that there are more knit
stitches than slipped stitches.

project: COLOR-STUDY COWL

Using slip-stitch is an excellent way to dip your toes into colorwork knitting. This chic bandana-shaped cowl makes use of the darkest color in the gradient, which is slip-stitched against a stockinette background using the lighter colors. Beginning with a traditional garter tab cast-on typically seen in shawl construction, the sport-weight cowl is worked flat, back and forth, and increased at the center and edges. Once the cowl has reached the optimal width, the work is joined in the round and finished with a classic i-cord bind off. Complete the look by adding a gradient fringe along the bottom front.

YOU WILL NEED

- **Yarn Weight: Sport**
- **Blend: 100% Superwash Merino**
- **Yardage: 60 yd. (54 m) skeins**
- **Colors: 6 colors, C1–C6 (darkest to lightest)**
- **Needle: US size 5 (3.75 mm) circular needle (or size needed to obtain gauge), 20 in. (50 cm) long**
- **Tapestry needle**
- **3 stitch markers**

Gauge: 24 sts and 34 rows = 4 in. (10 cm) in blocked stockinette stitch

Approximate Finished Size: Neck opening: 22 in. (56 cm); Center-front: 15 in. (38 cm); Center-back: 6¾ in. (17 cm)

PATTERN NOTES

- The cowl is worked from the top down and center-front out, beginning with a garter-stitch tab that is cast on in a similar way to many top-down shawls. Take care not to work your first and last three stitches of each row too tightly, so that the neck opening of the cowl remains stretchy.

- You will be knitting a 3-st garter border with increases at the beginning and end of every row on the RS and WS, and on each side of the center stitch on the RS only.

- When the selvage (top edge) reaches approximately 22 in. (56 cm), you will join in the round.

- Increases continue at each side of the center st every other round to the bottom of the cowl, creating a bandana shape.

- I-cord bind-off finishes the bottom edge, and there is an optional fringe.

TO MAKE THE COWL

Using C2 (second darkest shade in the gradient set), CO 3 sts and knit 6 rows (3 garter ridges).

Next Row: K3, rotate work 90 degrees clockwise, and pick up and k 3 sts along the selvage edge (1 in each garter ridge). Rotate work again by 90 degrees clockwise and pick up and knit 1 st in each CO st. (9 sts)

SECTION 1
Row 1 (WS): K2, kfb, [p1, pm] two times, p1, kfb, k2. (11 sts)

Row 2 (RS): K2, kfb, k to marker, M1R, sm, k1, M1L, k to last 3 sts, kfb, k2. (4 sts inc)

Row 3 (WS): K2, kfb, p to last 3 sts, kfb, k2. (2 sts inc)

Repeat last 2 rows 17 more times. (119 sts)

Break C2.

Row 38 (RS): Join C1 (darkest shade in the gradient set), k2, kfb, sl 2 wyib, [k4, sl 2 wyib] to marker, M1R, sm, k1, sm, M1L, [sl 2 wyib, k4] to last 5 sts, sl 2 wyib, kfb, k2. (123 sts)

Row 39 (WS): K2, kfb, p1, sl 2 wyif, [p4, sl 2 wyif] to 1 st before marker, [p1, sm] two times, p1, [sl 2 wyif, p4] to last 6 sts, sl 2 wyif, p1, kfb, k2. (125 sts)

Row 40: K2, kfb, k2, sl 2 wyib, [k4, sl 2 wyib] to 1 st before marker, k1, M1R, sm, k1, sm, M1L, k1, [sl 2 wyib, k4] to last 7 sts, sl 2 wyib, k2, kfb, k2. (129 sts)

Row 41: K2, kfb, p3, sl 2 wyif, [p4, sl 2 wyif] to 2 sts before marker, p2, sm, p1, sm, p2, [sl 2 wyif, p4] to last 8 sts, sl 2 wyif, p3, kfb, k2. (131 sts)

Break C1.

Row 42 (RS): Join C3 (third color in the gradient set), k2, kfb, k1, sl 2 wyib, [k4, sl 2 wyib] to 5 sts before marker, k5, M1R, sm, sl 1 wyib, sm, M1L, k5, [sl 2 wyib, k4] to last 6 sts, sl 2 wyib, k1, kfb, k2. (135 sts)

Row 43 (WS): K2, kfb, p2, sl 2 wyif, [p4, sl 2 wyif] to 6 sts before marker, p6, sm, sl 1 wyif, sm, p6, [sl 2 wyif, p4] to last 7 sts, sl 2 wyif, p2, kfb, k2. (137 sts)

Row 44: K2, kfb, k3, sl 2 wyib, [k4, sl 2 wyib] to 6 sts before marker, k6, M1R, sm, sl 1 wyib, sm, M1L, k6, [sl 2 wyib, k4] to last 8 sts, sl 2 wyib, k3, kfb, k2. (141 sts)

Row 45: K2, kfb, p4, sl 2 wyif, [p4, sl 2 wyif] to 7 sts before marker, p7, sm, sl 1 wyif, sm, p7, [sl 2 wyif, p4] to last 9 sts, sl 2 wyif, p4, kfb, k2. (143 sts)

Continuing with C3, repeat rows 2 and 3 five more times. (173 sts)

Row 46 (RS): K2, kfb, k to marker, M1R, sm, k1, M1L, k to last 3 sts, kfb, k2, using a backward loop method, CO 1 st on right needle, pm, CO 1 more st. (179 sts)

The marker just placed will mark the beginning of the round. Join work in the round and k to the end of the round. (179 sts—89 on each side of the center st)

KNIT IN THE ROUND
Round 1: Knit to marker, M1R, sm, k1, M1L, knit to end of round. (2 sts inc)

Round 2: Knit.

Repeat rounds 1 and 2 once more. (183 sts)

Break C3.

Round 5: Join C1 (darkest shade in the gradient set), sl 1 wyib, [k4, sl 2 wyib] to marker, M1R, sm, k1, sm, M1L, [sl 2 wyib, k4] to last st, sl 1 wyib. (185 sts)

Round 6: Sl 1 wyib, [k4, sl 2 wyib] to 1 st before marker, [k1, sm] two times, k1, [sl 2 wyib, k4] to last st, sl 1 wyib.

Round 7: Sl 1 wyib, [k4, sl 2 wyib] to 1 st before marker, k1, M1R, sm, k1, sm, M1L, k1, [sl 2 wyib, k4] to last st, sl 1 wyib. (187 sts)

Round 8: Sl 1 wyib, [k4, sl 2 wyib] to 2 sts before marker, k2, sm, k1, sm, k2, [sl 2 wyib, k4] to last st, sl 1 wyib. Break C1.

Round 9: Join C4 (fourth color in the gradient set), k2, [sl 2 wyib, k4] to 7 sts before marker, sl 2 wyib, k5, M1R, sm, k1, sm, M1L, k5, [sl 2 wyib, k4] to last 4 sts, sl 2 wyib, k2. (189 sts)

Round 10: K2, [sl 2 wyib, k4] to 8 sts before marker, sl 2 wyib, k6, sm, k1, sm, k6, [sl 2 wyib, k4] to last 4 sts, sl 2 wyib, k2.

Round 11: K2, [sl 2 wyib, k4] to 8 sts before marker, sl 2 wyib, k6, M1R, sm, k1, sm, M1L, k6, [sl 2 wyib, k4] to last 4 sts, sl 2 wyib, k2. (191 sts)

Round 12: K2, [sl 2 wyib, k4] to 9 sts before marker, sl 2 wyib, k7, sm, k1, sm, k7, [sl 2 wyib, k4] to last 4 sts, sl 2 wyib, k2.

Repeat rounds 1 and 2 five more times. (201 sts)

Break C4.

Round 23: Join C1, k2, [sl 2 wyib, k4] to 2 sts before marker, sl 2 wyib, M1R, sm, k1, sm, M1L, [sl 2 wyib, k4] to last 4 sts, sl 2 wyib, k2. (203 sts)

Round 24: K2, [sl 2 wyib, k4] to 3 sts before

marker, sl 2 wyib, [k1, sm] two times, k1, [sl 2 wyib, k4] to last 4 sts, sl 2 wyib, k2.

Round 25: K2, [sl 2 wyib, k4] to 3 sts before marker, sl 2 wyib, k1, M1R, sm, k1, sm, M1L, k1, [sl 2 wyib, k4] to last 4 sts, sl 2 wyib, k2. (205 sts)

Round 26: K2, [sl 2 wyib, k4] to 4 sts before marker, sl 2 wyib, k2, sm, k1, sm, k2, [sl 2 wyib, k4] to last 4 sts, sl 2 wyib, k2. Break C1.

Round 27: Join C5 (fifth color in the gradient set), sl 1 wyib, [k4, sl 2 wyib] to 5 sts before marker, k5, M1R, sm, sl 1 wyib, sm, M1L, k5, [sl 2 wyib, k4] to last st, sl 1 wyib. (207 sts)

Round 28: Sl 1 wyib, [k4, sl 2 wyib] to 6 sts before marker, k6, sm, sl 1 wyib, sm, k6, [sl 2 wyib, k4] to last st, sl 1 wyib.

Round 29: Sl 1 wyib, [k4, sl 2 wyib] to 6 sts before marker, k6, M1R, sm, sl 1 wyib, sm, M1L, k6, [sl 2 wyib, k4] to last st, sl 1 wyib. (209 sts)

Round 30: Sl 1 wyib, [k4, sl 2 wyib] to 7 sts before marker, k7, sm, sl 1 wyib, sm, k7, [sl 2 wyib, k4] to last st, sl 1 wyib.

Repeat rounds 1 and 2 five more times. (219 sts)

Break C5.

Round 41: Join C1, sl 1 wyib, [k4, sl 2 wyib] to marker, M1R, sm, k1, sm, M1L, [sl 2 wyib, k4] to last st, sl 1 wyib. (221 sts)

Round 42: Sl 1 wyib, [k4, sl 2 wyib] to 1 st before marker, [k1, sm] two times, k1, [sl 2 wyib, k4] to last st, sl 1 wyib.

Round 43: Sl 1 wyib, [k4, sl 2 wyib] to 1 st before marker, k1, M1R, sm, k1, sm, M1L, k1, [sl 2 wyib, k4] to last st, sl 1 wyib. (223 sts)

Round 44: Sl 1 wyib, [k4, sl 2 wyib] to 2 st before marker, k2, sm, k1, sm, k2, [sl 2 wyib, k4] to last st, sl 1 wyib. Break C1.

Round 45: Join C6 (sixth color in the gradient set), k2, [sl 2 wyib, k4], to 7 sts before marker, sl 2 wyib, k5, M1R, sm, k1, sm, M1L, k5, [sl 2 wyib, k4] to last 4 sts, sl 2 wyib, k2. (225 sts)

Round 46: K2, [sl 2 wyib, k4], to 8 sts before marker, sl 2 wyib, k6, sm, k1, sm, k6, [sl 2 wyib, k4] to last 4 sts, sl 2 wyib, k2.

Round 47: K2, [sl 2 wyib, k4], to 8 sts before marker, sl 2 wyib, k6, M1R, sm, k1, sm, M1L, k6, [sl 2 wyib, k4] to last 4 sts, sl 2 wyib, k2. (227 sts)

Round 48: K2, [sl 2 wyib, k4], to 9 sts before marker, sl 2 wyib, k7, sm, k1, sm, k7, [sl 2 wyib, k4] to last 4 sts, sl 2 wyib, k2.

Repeat rounds 1 and 2 three more times. (233 sts)

I-CORD BIND OFF
CO 2 sts using Cable CO method (see page 120). *K2, k2tog tbl, sl 3 sts from right needle back to left needle. Pull yarn across the back; rep from * until 3 sts remain. Finish by either k1, k2tog tbl, sl 2 sts to left needle, k2tog OR by grafting the last 3 sts to the first three sts of the i-cord bind off.

FINISHING

Weave in all loose ends with tapestry needle. If desired, add a six-strand fringe to the bottom edge spaced every sixth bound-off st and trim to 1½ in. (4 cm) length. Block to measurements.

Lesson 3: Alternating Stripes

Striping is the best way to experience and practice knitting with more than one color for the first time. By combining two or more yarns with the same gauge and yarn weight, you can add depth and playfulness, and make any project more graphic.

When using multiple colors, the color not in use can be left at the beginning of the row or round. Once the desired thickness of stripe has been reached, the new color can be picked up from behind and worked, leaving the other color in its place. When working thicker stripes, the yarn can be carried up the side of the work, alleviating the need to cut the yarn after each stripe and weave in many ends.

When knitting stripes in the round, a "stair step" will occur as a result of the nature of circular knitting. This can be eliminated by using the jogless stripe technique, which forces the stair step to drop down on an even field with the remainder of the stripe.

An extra element of interest can be added by knitting on the bias (as shown opposite). Striping on a diagonal appears difficult, but by adding stitches and taking them away at the end or beginning of the rows, an oblique line is formed, and the knitting will continue to keep a rectangular or square shape. Working with multiple colors in highly contrasting shades can further enhance this effect.

1 When beginning a stripe with the
... next color on the right side of the
work, bring the new color strand
up and behind the most recently
worked color strand. Insert the
right-hand needle into the first
stitch to knit.

2 Fully execute the knit stitch with the
... new color.

3 Bring the yarn to the front to make a
... yarn over.

4 Continue knitting with the new color to the
··· end of the row.

5 Flip the work and begin a new wrong-side
··· row. Knit the first stitch.

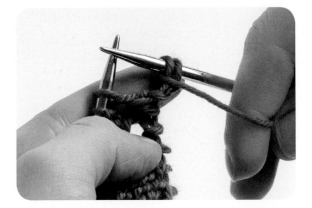

6 When making a yarn over on the wrong side
··· that is directly followed by a purl stitch, the
yarn must be brought to the front between
the two needles, then wrapped completely
around the right-hand needle 360 degrees.
The yarn should end up back in the front.

7 Purl the next stitch.
···

8 Purl to the end of the row.
···

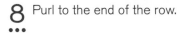

project: STRIPEY BLANKET

What's better than working with one gradient yarn? Working with two gradient yarns! This design brings together two different Aran-weight gradient hues in an effortless stockinette stitch striped repeat, creating not only an interesting color pattern within a color pattern but also—by knitting on the bias—creating an attractive diagonal stripe motif with simple increases and decreases. The edges are then finished off with a garter border. Knit in a portable size, this project would also work well as a baby stroller blanket. This is a fine example of letting the yarn do the work for you; this project looks more complex than it is, and truly celebrates gradient yarns.

YOU WILL NEED

- **Yarn Weight: Aran**
- **Blend: 100% Superwash Merino**
- **Yardage: 130 yd. (119 m), 2½ oz. (70 g)**
- **Colors: 3 balls in gradient yarn (A); 2 balls in gradient yarn (B)**
- **Needles: US size 7 (4.5 mm) circular needle, 24 in. (60 cm) long; US size 6 (4 mm) circular needle, 60 in. (150 cm) long (or sizes needed to obtain gauge)**
- **8 stitch markers**
- **Tapestry needle**

Gauge: 14 sts and 26 rows = 4 in. (10 cm) in stockinette striped pattern on larger needles

Approximate Finished Size: 25 in. (63.5 cm) wide by 45 in. (114.5 cm) long, blocked

TO MAKE THE BLANKET

INCREASE SLANTED EDGE
Using A and larger needle, CO 3 sts.

Knit 1 row.

Row 1 (RS): With B, k1, yo, knit to end. (1 st inc)

Row 2 (WS): K1, yo, purl to last st, k1. (1 st inc)

Row 3: With A, k1, yo, knit to end. (1 st inc)

Row 4: K1, yo, purl to last st, k1. (1 st inc)

Continue working rows 1–4 in stripe pattern 23 more times, then work rows 1 and 2 again. (101 sts)

DIAGONAL
Row 5 (RS): With A, k1, yo, knit to end. (1 st inc)

Row 6 (WS): K1, p2tog, purl to last st, k1. (1 st dec)

Row 7: With B, k1, yo, knit to end. (1 st inc)

Row 8: K1, p2tog, purl to last st, k1. (1 st dec)

Continue working rows 5–8 in stripe pattern until short straight edge measures 22 in. (56 cm), ending with row 8. Stitch count will remain at 101 after each repeat.

DECREASE SLANTED EDGE
Row 9 (RS): With A, k1, k2tog, knit to end. (1 st dec)

Row 10 (WS): K1, p2tog, purl to last st, k1. (1 st dec)

Row 11: With B, k1, k2tog, knit to end. (1 st dec)

Row 12: K1, p2tog, purl to last st, k1. (1 st dec)

Continue working rows 9–12 in stripe pattern 23 more times, then work rows 9 and 10 again. (3 sts)

Bind off remaining sts.

BORDER
Using A and smaller needle, starting at one corner, [pick up and knit 100 sts along short edge, pm, k1, pm, pick up and knit 194 sts along long edge, pm, k1, pm] twice. (592 sts.) Join into the round.

Next Round: Purl.

Next Round: [Knit to marker, yo, sm, k1, sm, yo] four times. (8 sts inc)

Next Round: Purl.

Repeat last 2 rounds once more.

Next Round: [Knit to marker, yo, sm, k1, sm, yo] four times. (616 sts)

Bind off all sts loosely purlwise.

FINISHING

Weave in all loose ends with tapestry needle. Block to measurements.

Lesson 4: Thrumming

Thrumming is a technique that dates back hundreds of years. It originated in the Labrador and Newfoundland areas of northeastern Canada, where temperatures dip far below freezing in the winter months. Thrumming adds an extra layer of warmth, unlike any other knitting technique.

Thrumming is mostly used in smaller garments such as mittens, hats, and socks. The term "thrum" once referred to the waste yarn left over from knitting looms, but instead of throwing the waste away, knitters worked these bits of yarn into their projects, creating a soft inner layer that made the fabric impenetrable by wind or cold and trapped body heat inside, much like a down blanket does.

While modern knitters use small pieces of unspun wool, or roving, in lieu of yarn waste, the process of working these bits into the knitting remains largely the same. By pulling apart small sections of roving—no wider than a finger—and gently stretching and fluffing them out, tiny air pockets are added to the fiber, which trap body heat inside a garment. Folding and knitting the roving directly into the work by piggybacking onto a stitch ensures that it stays in place.

Over time, the inside of the thrummed project felts slightly because of body heat, sweat, and friction, turning the roving into a more consistent inner layer. When choosing roving, it is important to use a 100 percent animal fiber that has not been treated to be machine washable. This will allow the felting process to occur.

Thrums can be placed in a project randomly or worked in as part of a pattern. Embrace a boldly hand-dyed roving to play off the yarn, or gravitate toward natural colors. Either way, thrumming is a tried and true, beautiful, and practical way to stay warm.

1 ... Divide the braid of animal fiber roving into chunks 8 in. (20 cm) in length. From these smaller chunks, carefully pull apart pieces no wider than ½ in. (1.25 cm).

2 ... Gently stretch the smaller pieces of roving by pulling at both ends. Adding length and aerating the roving will provide more warmth to the mittens.

3 Fold both ends of the stretched roving piece inward to form a bowtie shape, making sure the ends slightly overlap.

4 Quickly rub the bowtie back and forth in your hands to flatten the ends down. The heat and friction created will keep the ends from popping out. You now have a completed thrum.

5 Following the pattern, knit to where a thrum should be placed. Insert the right-hand needle into the stitch to be thrummed.

6 Fold the thrum in half over the needle, making sure the ends face inward to the wrong side of the work.

7 Loop the working yarn around the stitch to
... be thrummed and pull the knit stitch through,
making sure both the working yarn and
the thrum have been caught and are held
together, fully executing the stitch.

8 Knit to the next stitch that needs to
... be thrummed.

9 The wrong side of the
... work may look chaotic, but
with only a bit of wear, the
heat and friction from your
hands will felt down the
roving, creating a uniform
layer of warm thrums
that will not let cold or
wind through.

project: THRUMMED MITTENS

There is nothing warmer than a pair of thrummed mittens. Made in the round from the bottom up on double-pointed needles, with an afterthought thumb, these worsted-weight mitts are designed to keep the warmth in and the chill out. Small bits of solid-colored roving (unspun yarn) are folded and knitted in with the gradient yarn at charted intervals, creating an incredibly lush and soft inner layer. The finished appearance is that of an oversized mitten with bits of fluffy texture. Once you knit and wear a pair of thrummed mittens, you'll never want to wear anything else!

YOU WILL NEED

- Yarn Weight: Aran and roving
- Blend: Aran yarn: 45% Silk, 35% Merino Wool, 20% Nylon; Roving: 100% Falkland Wool
- Yardage: 220 yd. (200 m), 3½ oz. (100 g); 4 oz. (115 g) braid of roving
- Colors: 1 ball of gradient yarn and 1 braid 100% Falkland Wool for roving
- Needles: US size 8 (5 mm) DPNs (or size needed to obtain gauge)
- Stitch markers
- Waste yarn
- Tapestry needle

Gauge: 14 sts and 21 rows = 4 in. (10 cm) in thrummed pattern in the round

Approximate Finished Size: One size fits most adult women. Palm circumference 11 in. (28 cm) by 10½ in. (27 cm) length

TO MAKE THE MITTENS

CUFF

Using German Twisted CO method (see page 119), CO 36 sts. Join into round, being careful not to twist sts, pm for beginning of round.

Work in k2, p2 rib for 15 rounds or 2½ in. (6.5 cm).

Next Round: [K8, kfb] four times. (40 sts)

BODY OF MITT

Knit 2 rounds. Begin chart, working rounds 1–8 twice.

Next Round: While continuing in thrum pattern (see chart), work 7 sts, slip these 7 sts to waste yarn, and continue in pattern to end of round. (33 sts)

Next Round: Backward loop CO 7 sts, continue in pattern to end of round. (40 sts)

Continue even until work measures 10½ in. (26.5 cm) from CO edge, ending after a thrummed round.

TOP OF HAND DECREASES

Next Round: [K2tog, k1] to last st, k1. (27 sts)

Knit 1 round.

Next Round: [K2tog, k1] to end of round. (18 sts)

Next Round: [Thrum, k2] to end of round.

Next Round: [K2tog, k1] to end of round. (12 sts)

Knit 1 round.

Next Round: [K2tog, k1] to end of round. (8 sts)

Break yarn, weave through remaining sts. Pull tight to close and secure on WS.

THUMB

Pick up 7 sts from waste yarn, 1 st in gap, 7 sts from CO thumb edge, 1 st in gap. Join into round, and pm for beginning of round. (16 sts)

Knit 2 rounds.

Begin on round 5 of chart and work until thumb measures 2½ in. (6.5 cm)

Next Round: [K1, k2tog] to last st, k1. (11 sts)

Knit 1 round.

Next Round: [K2tog] to last st, k1. (6 sts)

Break yarn, weave through remaining sts. Pull tight to close and secure on WS.

FINISHING

Weave in all loose ends with a tapestry needle. Block lightly.

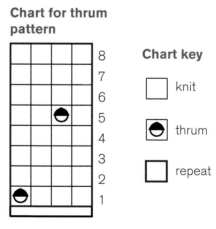

Chart for thrum pattern

Rep these 4 sts

Chart key

□ knit

⬤ thrum

□ repeat

Lesson 5: Cabling

Believed to have originated in the Aran Islands off the western coast of Ireland, and possibly inspired by the stunning scrollwork and art featured in the famous *Book of Kells*, cable knitting creates a warm, textured fabric often referred to as "Aran knitting."

Living in a remote part of Ireland meant warmth was a priority. While many of the men were at sea fishing, most women stayed on the island, raising children and knitting for their families and the traders who stopped by. Using wool spun from the island sheep resulted in a more rustic yarn that retained the natural lanolin from the animal, making the fiber waterproof, extra warm, and capable of providing the excellent stitch definition required for cabling.

Basic cable construction is the simple act of working stitches in a pattern out of order. By overlapping stitches at charted intervals, both simple and complex patterns will emerge, creating a three-dimensional effect and a double-thick fabric at the crossings. Often tucked among the cables are other raised stitches, such as bobbles that look like popcorn, or diamond motifs comprised of cables with seed- or moss-stitch centers for added texture.

This technique is ideal for sweaters and accessories alike, and is often seen in stores, which is a nod to its worldwide popularity.

1 Work in pattern to a 2/2 RC cable. Slip the next two stitches on the left-hand needle purlwise onto the cable needle. Hold the cable needle to the back of the work.

2 Keeping the cable needle at the back of the work, knit the next two stitches on the left-hand needle.

3 Bring the cable needle to the front of the work and knit the two slipped stitches directly off the cable needle and onto the right-hand ncedle.

4 This creates a right-leaning 4-stitch cable.

5 Work in pattern to a 2/2 LC cable. Slip the next two stitches on the left-hand needle purlwise onto the cable needle. Hold the cable needle to the front of the work.

6 Keeping the cable needle to the front of the work, knit the next two stitches on the left-hand needle. Knit the two slipped stitches directly off the cable needle and onto the right-hand needle.

7 This creates a left-leaning 4-stitch cable.

project: GRADIENT BLOCK COWL

Worked in a squashy, chunky-weight yarn, this cabled infinity cowl is ideal for warding off the winter chill while also adding a versatile accessory to your wardrobe. Started with a provisional cast-on and finished off with kitchener stitch for a seamless look, this large cable pattern, worked in consistent solids against a gradient stockinette background, creates a highly contrasting texture. This project is worked back and forth on circular needles to accommodate the large number of stitches. Double moss-stitch sections add length, allowing the wearer to sport it long for a modern look or wrapped around the neck twice for extra coziness.

YOU WILL NEED

- **Yarn Weight: Aran**
- **Blend: 100% Superwash Merino**
- **Yardage: 275 yd. (251 m), 8 oz. (228 g) for MC1 and MC2; 72 yd. (66 m), 2 oz. (60 g) each for CC1–CC5**
- **Colors: 2 skeins for MC1 and MC2, 1 set (5 mini skeins) for CC1, CC2, CC3, CC4, CC5**
- **Needle: US size 10 (6 mm) circular needles (or size needed to obtain gauge) 24 in. (60 cm) long**
- **Tapestry needle**
- **Crochet hook**

Gauge: 16 sts and 25 rows = 4 in. (10 cm) in double moss stitch after blocking; 1 repeat of cable pattern (8 sts and 12 rows) after blocking = approximately 1¾ in. (4.5 cm) wide and 1½ in. (4 cm) high

Approximate Finished Size: Circumference: 61 in. (155 cm); Height: 11¾ in. (30 cm)

SLIPPED STITCH EDGE (SSE)

RS Rows: K1, sl 1 wyif, k1.

WS Rows: Sl 1 wyif, k1, sl 1 wyif.

CABLE PATTERN

Row 1 (RS): SSE, *k5, drop yo, [sl 1 wyib] twice, drop yo, k1; rep from * to last 3 sts, SSE.

Row 2 (WS): SSE, *k1, [sl 1 wyif] twice, k5; rep from * to last 3 sts, SSE.

Row 3: SSE, *k5, [sl 1 wyib] twice, k1; rep from * to last 3 sts, SSE.

Row 4: Repeat row 2.

Row 5: SSE, *k3, 2/2 RC, k1; rep from * to last 3 sts, SSE.

Row 6: SSE, *p5, yo, p2, yo, p1; rep from * to last 3 sts, SSE.

Row 7: SSE, *k1, drop yo, [sl 1 wyib] twice, drop yo, k5; rep from * to last 3 sts, SSE.

Row 8: SSE, *k5, [sl 1 wyif] twice, k1; rep from * to last 3 sts, SSE.

Row 9: SSE, *k1, s1 wyib twice, k5; rep. from * to last 3 sts, SSE.

Row 10: Repeat row 8.

Row 11: SSE, *k1, 2/2 LC, k3; rep from * to last 3 sts, SSE.

Row 12: SSE, *p1, yo, p2, yo, p5; rep from * to last 3 sts, SSE.

Repeat rows 1–12 for pattern.

TO MAKE THE COWL

Using CC1 and provisional CO method (see page 118), CO 48 sts.

Row 1 (RS): K1, p1, k1, p to last 3 sts, k1, p1, k1.

Row 2 (WS): Sl 1 wyif, k1, sl 1 wyif, k to last 3 sts, sl 1 wyif, k1, sl 1 wyif.

Change to MC1.

Row 3: SSE, *k4, m1, k3; rep from * to last sts, SSE. (54 sts)

Row 4: SSE, *p1, yo, p2, yo, p5; rep from * to last 3 sts, SSE.

CABLE PATTERN–SECTION 1

Change to CC1 and work rows 1–4 of cable pattern.

Change to MC1 and work rows 5–6 of cable pattern.

Change to CC1 and work rows 7–10 of cable pattern.

Change to MC1 and work rows 11–12 of cable pattern.

Repeat Section 1 five more times.

CABLE PATTERN—SECTION 2

Change to CC2 and work rows 1–4 of cable pattern.

Change to MC1 and work rows 5–6 of cable pattern.

Change to CC2 and work rows 7–10 of cable pattern.

Change to MC1 and work rows 11–12 of cable pattern.

Repeat Section 2 four more times.

CABLE PATTERN—SECTION 3

Change to CC3 and work rows 1–4 of cable pattern.

Change to MC1 and work rows 5–6 of cable pattern.

Change to CC3 and work rows 7–10 of cable pattern.

Change to MC1 and work rows 11–12 of cable pattern.

Repeat first half of Section 3 two more times.

Change to CC3 and work rows 1–4 of cable pattern.

Change to MC1 and work rows 5–6 of cable pattern.

Change to CC3 and work rows 7–10 of cable pattern.

Change to MC2 and work rows 11–12 of cable pattern.

CABLE PATTERN—SECTION 4

Change to CC4 and work rows 1–4 of cable pattern.

Change to MC2 and work rows 5–6 of cable pattern.

Change to CC4 and work rows 7–10 of cable pattern.

Change to MC2 and work rows 11–12 of cable pattern.

Repeat Section 4 two more times.

CABLE PATTERN—SECTION 5

Change to CC5 and work rows 1–4 of cable pattern.

Change to MC2 and work rows 5–6 of cable pattern.

Change to CC5 and work rows 7–10 of cable pattern.

Change to MC2 and work rows 11–12 of cable pattern.

Change to CC5 and work rows 1–4 of cable pattern.

Change to MC2 and work rows 5–6 of cable pattern.

Change to CC5 and work rows 7–10 of cable pattern.

Change to MC2 and work row 11 of cable pattern, then row 12 as follows:

Row 12: SSE, purl to last 3 sts, SSE.

Change to CC5.

Row 13 (RS): SSE, *k2, ssk, k4; rep from * to last 3 sts, SSE. (48 sts)

Row 14 (WS): SSE, knit to last 3 sts, SSE.

Rows 15 and 16: SSE, purl to last 3 sts, SSE.

DOUBLE MOSS STITCH– SECTION 6
Change to MC2.

Set Up Row (RS): SSE, knit to last 3 sts, SSE.

Row 1 (WS): SSE, *k2, p2; rep from * to last 5 sts, k2, SSE.

Row 2 (RS): SSE, *p2, k2; rep from * to last 5 sts, p2, SSE.

Row 3 (WS): SSE, *p2, k2; rep from * to last 5 sts, p2, SSE.

Row 4 (RS): SSE, *k2, p2; rep from * to last 5 sts, k2, SSE.

Repeat rows 1–4 until double moss stitch measures approximately 20½ in. (52 cm).

DOUBLE MOSS STITCH–SECTION 7

Change to MC1.

Set Up Row (WS): SSE, purl to last 3 sts, SSE.

Row 1 (RS): SSE, *p2, k2; rep from * to last 5 sts, p2, SSE.

Row 2 (WS): SSE, *k2, p2; rep from * to last 5 sts, k2, SSE.

Row 3 (RS): SSE, *k2, p2; rep from * to last 5 sts, k2, SSE.

Row 4 (WS): SSE, *p2, k2; rep from * to last 5 sts, p2, SSE.

Repeat rows 1–4 until double moss stitch measures approximately 10¼ in. (26 cm) from color change.

FINISHING

Break yarn, leaving tail approximately 32 in. (81.5 cm) long. Carefully remove provisional cast-on and place all stitches on spare needles. Graft all stitches together invisibly, using kitchener stitch (see page 122).

Weave in all loose ends with tapestry needle. Block lightly.

Cable pattern chart

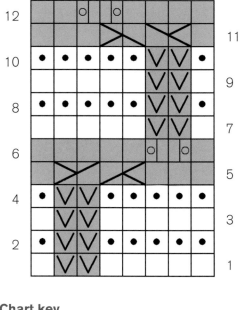

Chart key

☐	CC	☐	knit on RS; purl on WS
■	MC	•	purl on RS; knit on WS

sl 1 wyif on WS
sl 1 wyib on RS

yo, p1 (drop yo on next row)

p1, yo (drop yo on next row)

2/2 RC

2/2 LC

Lesson 6: Fair Isle

Situated where the North Sea and the Atlantic Ocean meet, the Shetlands are a group of small islands, only about a dozen of which are inhabited. The tenth largest of these is Fair Isle, where it is believed that stranded colorwork knitting originated. While the term "Fair Isle knitting" was initially reserved for those knitting stranded colorwork and residing on Fair Isle, it now enjoys a much broader definition, referring to anyone working this technique anywhere in the world.

While this technique can feature many colors, only two colors are used per round. Whether you are using brightly dyed, naturally dyed, or undyed yarn, both colors are carried across the round at the back, making a stranded, double-thick fabric. To avoid large loops of yarn on the wrong side of the work, which may get caught, yarn is "trapped" or "floated" at certain intervals, keeping both the outside and the inside of the work tidy. Fair Isle knitting may also be "steeked," or cut, allowing the knitter to work quickly in the round rather than back and forth.

This is the only knitting technique where the knitter can work "combination style," with the right hand "throwing" or knitting in the English style and the left hand "picking" or knitting in the Continental style. This enables speed and efficiency. Fair Isle is almost always accompanied by a chart.

1 Hold the nondominant, or foreground, color
... in the right hand and the dominant, or
background, color in the left hand. This is
referred to as "combination knitting."

2 Dominant stitches are worked Continental
... style with the left hand, naturally running
underneath the nondominant color.

3 Nondominant stitches are worked English
... style with the right hand, naturally running
above the nondominant color.

4 Using this method, naturally occurring "floats"
... are created on the wrong side of the work.
Take care not to pull the yarns too tightly or
the work will pucker.

project: FESTOON MITTENS

Begun with a stretchy cast-on and constructed from the bottom up with a ribbed cuff worked in the round, these fingering-weight Fair Isle mittens are designed in a traditional Scandinavian style. The mittens feature two different patterns: a diamond motif on the palm side that then transforms into floral garlands flanked by heraldic eagles on the top side. A darker, solid-colored background showcases the lighter gradient foreground, showing off the individual stitches. Unlike a traditional ombré-style gradient, this gradient set comes in a pre-matched, perfectly coordinating color scheme. A solid afterthought thumb is added on at the end.

YOU WILL NEED

- **Yarn Weight: Sock**
- **Blend: 80% Superwash Merino, 20% Nylon**
- **Yardage: 425 yd. (389 m) per 4 oz. (115 g) skein for MC; 105 yd. (96 m) per 1 oz. (30 g) skein for CC**
- **Colors: 1 skein for MC; 1 set of 5 mini-skeins for CC1, CC2, CC3, CC4, CC5**
- **Needle: US size 1 (2.25 mm) double-pointed needles (or size needed to obtain gauge)**
- **Tapestry needle**
- **Stitch marker**
- **12 in. (30.5 cm) piece of fingering-weight scrap yarn**

Gauge: 36 sts and 44 rounds = 4 in. (10 cm) in stranded colorwork pattern

Approximate Finished Size: Women's medium size. Palm circumference 8 in. (20.5 cm) by 9½ in. (24 cm) long

Color chart for mittens

Needle 4   Needle 3   Needle 2   Needle 1

Chart key

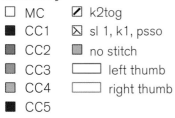

☐ MC	☑ k2tog	
■ CC1	⊠ sl 1, k1, psso	
■ CC2	■ no stitch	
■ CC3	▭ left thumb	
■ CC4	▭ right thumb	
■ CC5		

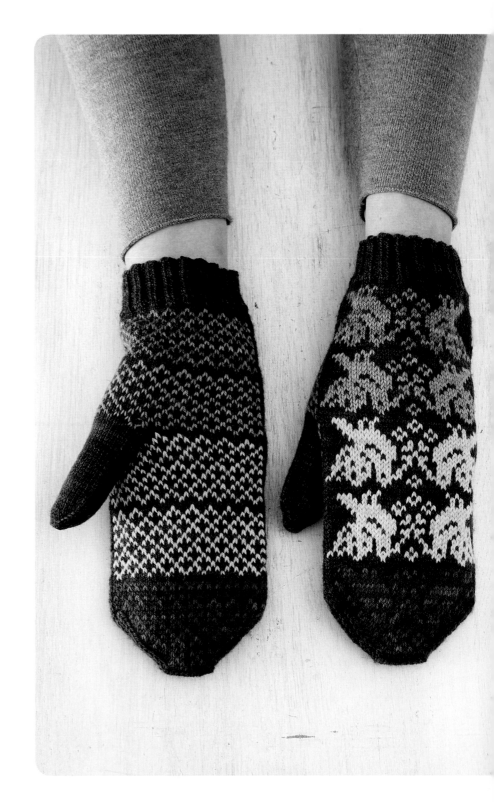

TO MAKE THE MITTENS

CUFF

Using MC, CO 72 sts using Long-Tail CO method (see page 117) or any other stretchy cast-on. Distribute sts evenly across 4 needles with 18 sts on each needle. The needles will now be known as N1, 2, 3, and 4, respectively. Join into round, being careful not to twist sts, pm for beginning of round.

Round 1: [K2 tbl, p2] around.

Rep round 1 for 11 more rounds.

Knit 2 rounds.

MITTEN BODY

Work rounds 1–31 from chart, reading each round from right to left.

THUMB PLACEMENT

For Left Mitten: Work in patt across N1, N2, and N3, then work first 3 sts on N4, knit the next 12 sts with scrap yarn, sl these sts back to LH needle, and work in patt to end of round.

For Right Mitten: Work in patt across N1 and N2, then first 3 sts on N3, knit the next 12 sts with scrap yarn, sl these sts back to LH needle and work in patt across rem sts on N3, and all sts on N4.

Cont working through round 72. Please note: The finger decs can be successfully executed working only from the chart or from the instructions below (or both).

FINGER DECREASES

Round 73: Dec for fingertips as foll:

N1: K1, sl 1, k1, psso, work across rem sts in patt;

N2: Work in patt to last 2 sts, k2tog;

N3: K1, sl 1, k1, psso, work across rem sts in patt;

N4: Work in patt to last 2 sts, k2tog. (4 sts dec)

Rep last round 12 more times, through round 85. (20 sts remain, with 5 sts on each needle)

Sl all sts from N2 to N1, and all sts from N4 to N3. (10 sts on each needle) Break MC, leaving an 18 in. (45.5 cm) long tail to graft remaining sts. Using tail, use kitchener stitch (see page 122) to join sts at top of mitten.

WORKING THE THUMB

Remove scrap yarn from thumb opening and place 24 sts on 4 needles, with 6 sts on each needle. With MC, begin at lower right needle, pick up 1 st in gap before N1, then k 6 sts on needle;

k 6 sts from N2 and pick up 1 st in gap at end of opening; pick up 1 st in gap before N3, then k 6 sts on needle; k 6 sts from N4 and pick up 1 st in gap at end of opening. (28 sts, with 7 sts on each needle)

Join into round, pm for beginning of round. Work thumb as foll:

Round 1: Knit.

Cont in stockinette stitch until thumb is ½ in. (1.2 cm) short of desired length.

WORKING THUMB DECREASES

Next round: Dec for top of thumb as foll:

N1: Sl 1, k1, psso, knit to end of needle;

N2: knit to last 2 sts, k2tog;

N3: sl 1, k1, psso, knit to end of needle;

N4: knit to last 2 sts, k2tog. (4 sts dec)

Rep last round 5 more times. (8 sts remain, with 2 sts on each needle)

Break yarn, leaving a tail approx 8 in. (20.5 cm) long. Draw tail through remaining sts twice and pull tight to close, and secure on WS.

FINISHING

Weave in all loose ends with a tapestry needle. Block to measurements.

Lesson 7: Intarsia

In a way similar to the woodworking technique, intarsia knitting creates blocks of color with the yarn. It differs from Fair Isle in that the yarns are not carried across the back to create a double-thick fabric; instead, yarn is worked in small amounts back and forth in sections.

When color changes occur in the same row, one yarn is left behind while the new color is picked up from underneath and worked, "linking" the yarns together. The result is that the back of the work looks similar to the front, with no holes at the color changes, creating a single layer of fabric. Intarsia is often seen in larger-scale garments, but can be used for projects of any size.

Most commonly seen when knitting Argyle or motifs with larger geometric blocks of color, rather than for all-over patterning like its cousin Fair Isle, intarsia is usually worked flat back and forth in rows. This project is worked back and forth on circular needles to accommodate the large number of stitches. Almost always charted, intarsia knitting is generally worked in stockinette or garter stitch.

1 On the right side of the work, knit to where
... the new color is to be picked up.

2 Twist the old color over and to the left of
... the new color. Bring the new color up to the
right of the old color. The old color will be left
hanging at the back where the colors were
switched and may need to be gently tugged
to even up the tension.

3 Knit to the end of the row with the new color.

4 On the wrong side of the work, knit to where the new color is to be picked up.

5 Bring up the old color between the needles to the front of the work and to the left.

6 Bring up the new color between the needles to the back of the work. The old color will be left hanging at the front where the colors were switched and may need to be gently tugged to even up the tension.

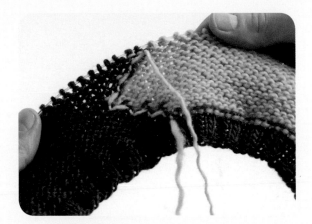

7 Begin knitting with the new color and
••• work to the end of the row, leaving the old
color hanging.

8 The wrong side of the work will have the
••• strands carried up along the join.

9 The right side of
••• the work will be
tidy, with no gaps
at the joins.

project: ZIGZAG LEGWARMERS

Knit yourself a pair of these playful, sport-weight legwarmers and you'll be an intarsia pro in no time! By using two balls of identical-gradient yarn worked from opposite ends, a dramatic graphic effect takes shape, combining both style and contrast. Worked from the top down, beginning with a twisted rib cuff and worked flat, back and forth in rows, the intarsia section is capped off with a matching cuff on the bottom edge. The work is then sewn into a tube with a mock opening added on the long edge, topped off with decorative, non-functional buttons. The right and left legwarmers are made in mirror-image to showcase the intarsia zigzag pattern.

YOU WILL NEED

- **Yarn Weight: Sport**
- **Blend: 100% Wool**
- **Yardage: 218 yd. (200 m), 2¾ oz. (75 g)**
- **Colors: 2 balls of ombré yarn, in same color**
- **Needle: US size 7 (4.5 mm) needles (or size needed to obtain gauge)**
- **6 locking stitch markers**
- **Tapestry needle**
- **Twelve ⅞ in. (22 mm) buttons**
- **Scrap yarn, preferably cotton**

Gauge: 20 sts and 36 rows = 4 in. (10 cm) in garter stitch, blocked

Approximate Finished Size: Circumference, excluding "opening" 12¼ in. (31 cm); Length 14½ in. (37 cm)

TO MAKE THE RIGHT LEGWARMER

With Ball A, CO 66 sts using Long-Tail CO method (see page 117).

TOP EDGE

Row 1 (RS): *P2, [k1 tbl] twice; rep from * to last 2 sts, p2.

Row 2 (WS): *K2, [p1 tbl] twice; rep from * to last 2 sts, k2.

Repeat rows 1 and 2 twice more.

ZIGZAG INTARSIA

Place a locking stitch marker on RS of work to keep track of right and wrong sides.

Row 1 (RS): With Ball A, k36, with Ball B, knit to end.

Row 2 (WS): With Ball B, k30, with Ball A, knit to end.

PATTERN NOTES

- This pattern is worked from the top edge down. It is worked flat and sewn into a tube at the end. It has a mock opening with non-functional buttons. The left and right legwarmers are worked from different instructions in order to mirror the colors and the zigzag pattern.

- Two balls of the same color of gradient yarn are used. The balls are worked from opposite ends. For each legwarmer, "Ball A" refers to the ball that is begun from the lighter end, and "Ball B" refers to the ball begun from the darker end. When working the second legwarmer, begin each ball from the end previously not used. This will create matching legwarmers.

- Twisting the yarns on mid-row color changes: Move the working yarn to the wrong side of the work (for some rows it will already be on the wrong side) and drop the working yarn to the left of the new color. Pick up the new color to the right of the old color, bring it from behind and over the old color, and into the correct position to begin working. This will twist the colors together on the wrong side. Always be sure to work the twist on the wrong side of the work. Place a locking stitch marker on the right side to help keep track of which side you are on.

Rows 3 and 4: Repeat rows 1 and 2.

Row 5: With Ball A, k34, with Ball B, knit to end.

Row 6: With Ball B, k32, with Ball A, knit to end.

Rows 7 and 8: Repeat rows 5 and 6.

Row 9: With Ball A, k32, with Ball B, knit to end.

Row 10: With Ball B, k34, with Ball A, knit to end.

Rows 11 and 12: Repeat rows 9 and 10.

Row 13: With Ball A, k30, with Ball B, knit to end.

Row 14: With Ball B, k36, with Ball A, knit to end.

Rows 15 and 16: Repeat rows 13 and 14.

Rows 17-20: Repeat rows 9–12.

Rows 21-24: Repeat rows 5–8.

Work rows 1–24 three more times, then work rows 1–14 again.

DECREASE
Row 1 (RS): With Ball A, (k3, k2tog) six times, with Ball B, k6, (ssk, k3) six times. (54 sts)

Row 2 (WS): With Ball B, k30, with Ball A, knit to end.

Break both yarns.

BOTTOM EDGE

Rejoin Ball B at beginning of row and work as follows.

Row 1 (RS): *P2, [k1 tbl] twice; rep from * to last 2 sts, p2.

Row 2 (WS): *K2, [p1 tbl] twice; rep from * to last 2 sts, k2.

Repeat rows 1 and 2 twice.

Bind off all sts in pattern.

TO MAKE THE LEFT LEGWARMER

With Ball A, CO 66 sts using Long-Tail CO method.

TOP EDGE

Row 1 (RS): *P2, [k1 tbl] twice; rep from * to last 2 sts, p2.

Row 2 (WS): *K2, [p1 tbl] twice; rep from * to last 2 sts, k2.

Repeat rows 1 and 2 twice.

Break Ball A.

ZIGZAG INTARSIA

Place a locking stitch marker RS of work to keep track of right and wrong sides.

Row 1 (RS): With Ball B, k30, with Ball A, knit to end.

Row 2 (WS): With Ball A, k36, with Ball B, knit to end.

Rows 3 and 4: Repeat rows 1 and 2.

Row 5: With Ball B, k32, with Ball A, knit to end.

Row 6: With Ball A, k34, with Ball B, knit to end.

Rows 7 and 8: Repeat rows 5 and 6.

Row 9: With Ball B, k34, with Ball A, knit to end.

Row 10: With Ball A, k32, with Ball B, knit to end.

Rows 11 and 12: Repeat rows 9 and 10.

Row 13: With Ball B, k36, with Ball A, knit to end.

Row 14: With Ball A, k30, with Ball B, knit to end.

Rows 15 and 16: Repeat rows 13 and 14.

Rows 17-20: Repeat rows 9–12.

Rows 21-24: Repeat rows 5–8.

Work rows 1–24 three more times, then work rows 1–14 again.

DECREASE

Row 1 (RS): With Ball B, (k3, k2tog) six times, k6, with Ball A, (ssk, k3) six times. (54 sts)

Row 2 (WS): With Ball A, k24, with Ball B, knit to end.

Break Ball A.

BOTTOM EDGE

With Ball B only, work as follows.

Row 1 (RS): *P2, [k1 tbl] twice; rep from * to last 2 sts, p2.

Row 2 (WS): *K2, [p1 tbl] twice; rep from * to last 2 sts, k2.

Repeat rows 1 and 2 twice more.

Bind off all sts in pattern.

FINISHING

BOTH LEGWARMERS

Weave in all loose ends with tapestry needle.
Steam block lightly (see page 134). Do not wet
block, as this may stretch the yarn and make the
legwarmers too large.

With WS facing, use a tapestry needle threaded
with piece of scrap yarn in a contrasting color, and
weave yarn through the stitch in each purl ridge
1 in. (2.5 cm) in from edge worked in Ball A (the
lighter-colored side). Continue through same line of
stitches in ribbing rows at top and bottom.

With WS facing, use line marked by scrap yarn as
guide to overlap edge worked in Ball B (dark edge)
1 in. (2.5 cm) over Ball A edge, and pin in place.

With leftover yarn from one of the balls, use whip
stitch to sew dark edge to light side along marked
line to leave 1 in. (2.5 cm) flap on RS of work that
simulates an opening. Take care not to catch scrap
yarn when sewing. Remove scrap yarn.

On RS, place six locking stitch markers, evenly
spaced, along "opening" of each legwarmer. Sew
buttons at marked locations, stitching through both
layers to secure the opening.

Lesson 8: Lace

"Lace" is often used as a general term for any knitting involving yarn overs and decreases. Producing a light and airy fabric, lace knitting is seen by some as an evolution of tatting, fretwork, and fine needlework, which was eventually adapted into a knitted form in the sixteenth century.

Lace knitting techniques hail mainly from Estonia, Shetland, and Orenburg. As for traditional Aran and Fair Isle knitting, many women would knit lace shawls for trade or profit, to contribute to the family income. Lace is considered by some to be the most complex knitting technique, and it is very difficult to replicate in machine knitting.

Passed down through oral tradition, many early Orenburg lace shawl motifs invoked nature, with patterns depicting trees, wildlife, and flowers. Worked using extremely fine mohair fiber, this type of lace knitting is often referred to as a "wedding ring shawl" because the entire shawl can be passed through a wedding ring–sized opening.

Shetland lace was favored by Queen Victoria and was very popular with knitters during her reign. Worked in fine fibers on tiny needles, this type of lace has yarn overs worked on both sides, making the knitting more challenging, as there isn't a resting row on the wrong side.

Estonian lace is often accompanied by "nupps," or raised bobble-like stitches, and scalloped edges, and is constructed in two pieces and sewn together in the middle.

Nowadays lace may be seen in all types of garments, using thicker, hand-dyed fibers for a more modern look. Shawl knitting enjoyed a renaissance in the early twenty-first century and remains popular.

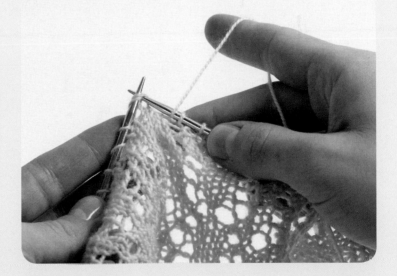

1 **...** When working row 1 of chart 1, knit two stitches and then bring the yarn between the needles and to the front of the work to yarn over.

2 **...** Insert the right-hand needle into the left of the next two stitches on the left-hand needle, putting the needle through both of them. Knit these two stitches together, creating a right-leaning decrease. Knit one stitch and then bring the yarn between the two needles to the front for another yarn over.

3 Begin the s2kp by slipping the next two
••• stitches from the left-hand needle to the
right-hand needle as if to k2tog, and then
knit 1 stitch.

4 With the left-hand needle, pick up the two
••• slipped stitches from the right-hand needle in
the front.

5 Pass the slipped stitches up and over the knit
••• stitch, then off the needle.

6 This creates a double decrease and forms the
••• apex of the lace triangle.

7 Bring the yarn between the needles to the front of the work for a yarn over and knit the next stitch.

8 Begin the ssk by slipping the next two stitches individually from the left-hand needle to the right-hand needle as if to knit.

9 Insert the left-hand needle into the front of the two slipped stitches on the right-hand needle and knit them together.

10 This creates a left-leaning decrease.

project: LACY STRIPE SHAWL

Cast on at the bottom edge and featuring four lace patterns that merge and flow into one another with each color shift, this fingering-weight shawl is a delicate and romantic accessory perfect for summer evenings. Once the lace portions are complete, the upper body of the shawl is worked back and forth in stockinette stitch and executed in the darkest color of the gradient. Easy, short rows create a crescent shape before a simple fifth lace section is added prior to binding off. Each color is worked until the yarn runs out, meaning the knitter will use almost every bit of yarn. Don't you just love it when that happens?

YOU WILL NEED

- **Yarn Weight: Fingering**
- **Blend: 100% Superwash Merino**
- **Yardage: 798 yd. (730 m), 7¾ oz. (220 g)**
- **Colors: 6-color set**
- **Needle: US size 5 (3.75 mm) circular needle, 40 in. (100 cm) long; US size 7 (4.5 mm) circular needle, 40 in. (100 cm) long (or size needed to obtain gauge)**
- **Tapestry needle**

Gauge: 22 sts and 40 rows = 4 in. (10 cm) in stockinette stitch on smaller needles

Approximate Finished Size: 62¼ in. (158 cm) wide by 13 in. (33 cm) deep

PATTERN NOTES

- This shawl is worked from the bottom up.

- It is very important to keep the cast-on edge loose. Go up a needle size if needed.

- There are no wrap and turns for the short rows; simply turn the work and begin working as instructed.

- When the work is turned to start a new short row, a gap between stitches is created. This gap is closed by a decrease.

- Work each of the first four colors in the gradient until you no longer have enough yarn to complete the next row. These colors will make up the lace edge.

- Work the body of the shawl in the fifth color of the gradient. You will have yarn remaining after completing the short rows.

- Work the top edge of the shawl in the sixth and final color of the gradient.

Lace chart 1

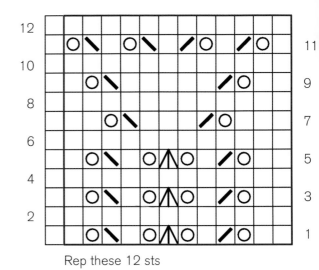

Rep these 12 sts

Lace chart 2

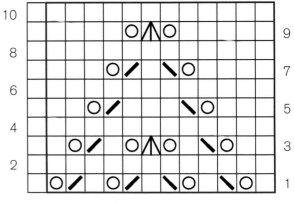

Rep these 12 sts

82   Lesson 8: Lace

Lace chart 3

Rep these 6 sts

Lace chart 4

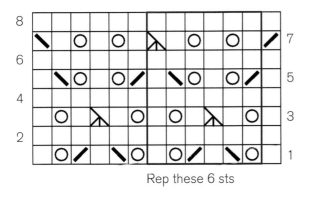

Rep these 6 sts

Lace chart 5

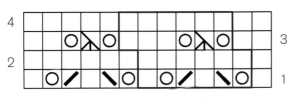

Rep these 6 sts

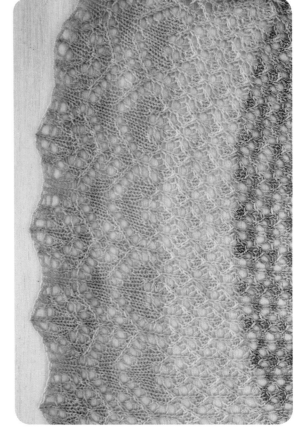

Charts key

☐	knit on RS rows / purl on WS rows	
◯	yo	
◮	s2kp	
╱	k2tog	
╲	ssk	
◪	sk2p	
☐	repeat	

TO MAKE THE SHAWL

Using larger needle and Knitted CO method (see page 116), CO 325 sts. Change to smaller needle.

Work rows 1–12 of Chart 1 once.

Work rows 1–10 of Chart 2 twice.

Work rows 1–2 of Chart 3 once.

Work rows 1–8 of Chart 4 three times.

Work rows 1–4 of Chart 5 four times.

Dec Row (RS): K1, *ssk, k1, k2tog, k1; rep from * to end of row. (217 sts)

Next Row (WS): Purl.

Work short rows as follows:

Short Row 1 (RS): K147, turn.

Short Row 2 (WS): P77, turn.

Short Row 3 (RS): Knit to 1 st before turning gap, ssk, k4, turn. (1 st dec)

Short Row 4 (WS): Purl to 1 st before turning gap, p2tog, p4, turn. (1 st dec)

Rep last 2 rows 13 more times. (189 sts)

Next Row (RS): K1, k2tog, k to last 3 sts, ssk, k1. (187 sts)

Next Row (WS): Purl.

Work rows 1–4 of Chart 5 once.

Knit 2 rows.

Bind off as follows: K2, *sl 2 sts back to left-hand needle, k2tog tbl, k1; rep from * until 1 st remains. Fasten off last st.

FINISHING

Weave in all loose ends with tapestry needle, but do not trim ends flush with work. Soak shawl in cool water for 20 minutes. Remove from water and gently squeeze. You may wish to roll the shawl in a large towel to remove as much water as possible. Pin shawl out to shape. Allow to dry thoroughly. Trim loose ends.

Lesson 9: Modular Knitting

First appearing in the 1940s, "number knitting," or what's more commonly referred to as modular knitting, is a technique akin to building with blocks, where new blocks are added onto an existing structure to make a larger piece.

Often constructed in rectangles and squares, triangles and diamonds, or curves, new blocks are added to the piece, creating "modules." New modules can be worked directly into existing ones, or multiple modules can be made and seamed together at the end with a border added on.

Worked in stockinette or garter stitch, this technique is often planned out on graph paper beforehand or worked in an improvised manner, much like a crazy quilt.

Modular designs work especially well in geometric-shaped projects such as blankets, bags, pillows, and scarves; however, modular knitting can be used creatively for garments and accessories as well.

Here, we're working back and forth on circular needles to accommodate the growing number of stitches used in the modular project.

1 When ready to add in a new color block, bind off the old color stitches along the edge, leaving the last stitch on the right-hand needle.

2 Turn the work by 90 degrees and pick up the garter bumps (one stitch for every two rows) along the side of the existing work.

3 Continue along the same edge, picking up one stitch in every bound-off stitch.

5 Slide the circular needle to the beginning of the picked-up edge and introduce the new color by knitting it directly into the work on the first stitch.

4 Pick up all stitches along the bound-off edge to the end of the existing work.

6 Continue knitting the picked-up stitches to the end of the row, then flip the work and knit back again, establishing the first row of the new color block.

project: MODULAR SCARF

Starting with a small garter-stitch rectangle, then built outward and upward in the modular knitting style, this striking unisex scarf is a statement piece for any knitter's wardrobe. Work it with bold colors as pictured, or tone it down with neutrals. With this technique, every bit of the gradient yarn can be used, and it's effortless to add or subtract sections to create a skinnier scarf or a more dramatic wrap. Finished off with a tidy border, this scarf is sure to garner attention.

YOU WILL NEED

- **Yarn Weight: DK**
- **Blend: 100% Superwash Merino**
- **Yardage: 140 yd. (128 m), 2 oz. (60 g) per skein**
- **Colors: 6 colors**
- **Needle: US size 8 (5 mm) circular needle (or size needed to obtain gauge), 32 in. (80 cm) long**
- **Tapestry needle**

Gauge: 18 sts and 34 rows = 4 in. (10 cm) in garter stitch

Approximate Finished Size: 11 in. (28 cm) wide by 74½ in. (189 cm) long, blocked

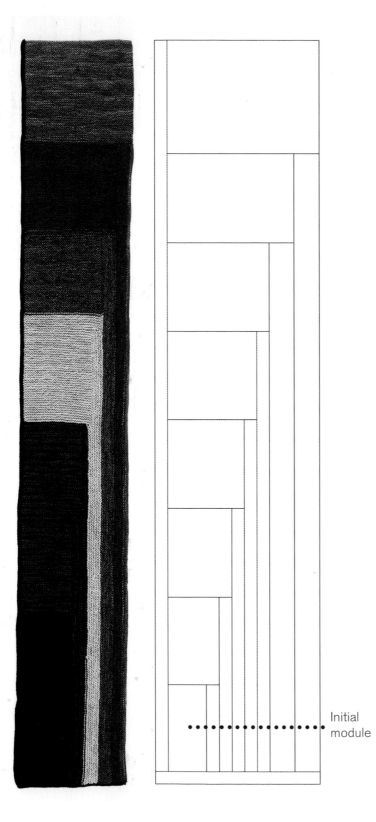

Initial
module

PATTERN NOTES

- Weigh the skein of the first color you are using as you work. When 1 oz. (30 g) remains, cut this color and join the next color. The remaining yarn will be used for the border.

- Except where indicated in the pattern, when you run out of a color, immediately join and begin working with the next color. For this reason, most color changes are not indicated in the pattern. The sections in the diagram will not necessarily coincide with color changes in your gradient. You can change colors on the right side of the project each time if you'd prefer to avoid the two-color "purl ridge" that results from changing color on the wrong side in garter stitch.

- Because this scarf is modular, you can use every inch of your gradient. You can also add or subtract modules to create a larger or smaller scarf.

TO MAKE THE SCARF

With first gradient color, and using Long-Tail CO method (see page 117), CO 20 sts.

Knit 79 rows. Bind off all sts, leaving last st on needle.

Turn work 90 degrees, pick up and k 40 sts along side edge (1 st for every 2 rows).

Knit 3 rows. Bind off all sts, leaving last st on needle.

RECTANGLE 1
Turn work 90 degrees, pick up and k 1 st in every 2 rows across edge of rows just worked, and 1 st in every st along bind-off edge. (22 sts)

Knit 79 rows. Bind off all sts and fasten off last st.

RECTANGLE 2
With RS facing, beg at south edge of piece, pick up and k 1 st for every st along bind-off edge and 1 st for every 2 rows along selvage edge. (80 sts)

Knit 7 rows. Bind off all sts, leaving last st on needle.

Repeat [Rectangle 1 and Rectangle 2] three more times, then work Rectangle 1 once more.

RECTANGLE 3
With RS facing, beg at bottom edge of piece, pick up and k 1 st for every st along bind-off edge and 1 st for every 2 rows along selvage edge. (240 sts)

Knit 11 rows. Bind off all sts, leaving last st on needle.

Repeat [Rectangle 1 and Rectangle 3] once more, then work Rectangle 1 until you run out of final gradient color.

BORDER
With RS facing and beg at top left corner of piece, using set aside first gradient color, pick up and k 1 st in every 2 rows along left edge of scarf.

Knit 1 row. Bind off all sts, leaving last st on needle.

Turn work 90 degrees, pick up and k 1 st in every st along CO portion of edge and 1 st in every 2 rows across selvage portion of bottom edge of scarf.

Knit 1 row. Bind off all sts. Fasten off last st.

FINISHING

Weave in all loose ends with tapestry needle. Block to measurements.

CARE
Although this yarn is superwash, it's advisable to wash it by hand or using the handwash cycle on your washing machine. Lay it flat to dry, and do not tumble dry.

Lesson 10: Wrap & Turn Short Rows

Short rows, sometimes called partial rows or turning rows, are used to lengthen or push out one particular portion of a knitted fabric. By working back and forth on one section of your knitting, adding in extra short rows, the fabric is lengthened in just that area, creating a wedge and a more properly fitting garment.

Short rows are commonly used for shaping shoulders, busts, sock heels, earflaps, and shawls. While there are countless types of short rows, such as the German, Japanese, yarn over, and many others, one of the simplest ways to work this technique is by using the popular wrap and turn technique. Other methods may create small holes in the finished work, giving the fabric a more jagged and unprofessional look. This method is the most common and is easy to do.

Slipping a stitch, wrapping the working yarn around that slipped stitch, slipping that same stitch back, then turning the work creates the wrap and turn short row. When the time comes to eliminate the wrapped stitch to remove the horizontal bars and make the work tidier, the wrap is simply picked up, placed on the left-hand needle, and knit together with the stitch, closing any gaps or holes. This elegant short row is both easy and consistent, making it perfect for any garment requiring short rows.

1 Work in pattern to the next wrap and turn.
... Slip the next stitch on the left-hand needle
purlwise to the right-hand needle.

2 Bring the yarn between the needles to the
... front of the work.

3 Slip the stitch on the
... right-hand needle back
over to the left-hand
needle.

4 Bring the yarn between the needles to the back of the work.

5 Turn the work to the wrong side. The yarn will be at the front.

6 Purl across the wrong side to the next stitch to be wrapped and turned.

7 Bring the yarn to the back of the work.

8 Slip the stitch on the right-hand needle back over to the left-hand needle.

9 Bring the yarn between the needles to the front of the work.

10 Continue in pattern until six stitches remain between the wrap and turn sections. Use the right-hand needle to pick up the front loop of the wraps on the right side.

11 Place the picked-up wrap onto the left-hand needle.

12 Knit the picked-up wrap and the next stitch together.

13 Use the right-hand needle to pick up the back loop of the wrap on the wrong side. Place the picked-up wrap on the left-hand needle.

14 Purl the picked-up wrap and the next stitch together.

project: MOTH SOCKS

These cozy handmade socks incorporate a Fair Isle moth motif. Worked in a large, 15-color palette, maintaining the color order is essential to keeping the gradient effect intact. Worked from the top down, starting with a ribbed cuff, the Fair Isle motif appears only on the body of the sock before a wrap and turn short row heel is turned. Finished off using only the background color with the kitchener stitch at the toes makes this project quick work.

YOU WILL NEED

- Yarn Weight: Fingering
- Blend: 80% Superwash Merino, 20% Nylon
- Yardage: 450 yd. (411 m) per 4¼ oz. (120 g) skein
- Colors: Gradient yarn set of 15 colors divided into two sets for each sock (see pattern notes on page 101 for detailed instructions)
- Needle: US size 2 (2.75 mm) double-pointed needles (or size needed to obtain gauge)
- Tapestry needle
- Stitch marker

Gauge: 32 sts and 32 rounds = 4 in. (10 cm) in stranded colorwork pattern

Approximate Finished Size: Women's medium. Foot circumference 8 in. (20.5 cm)

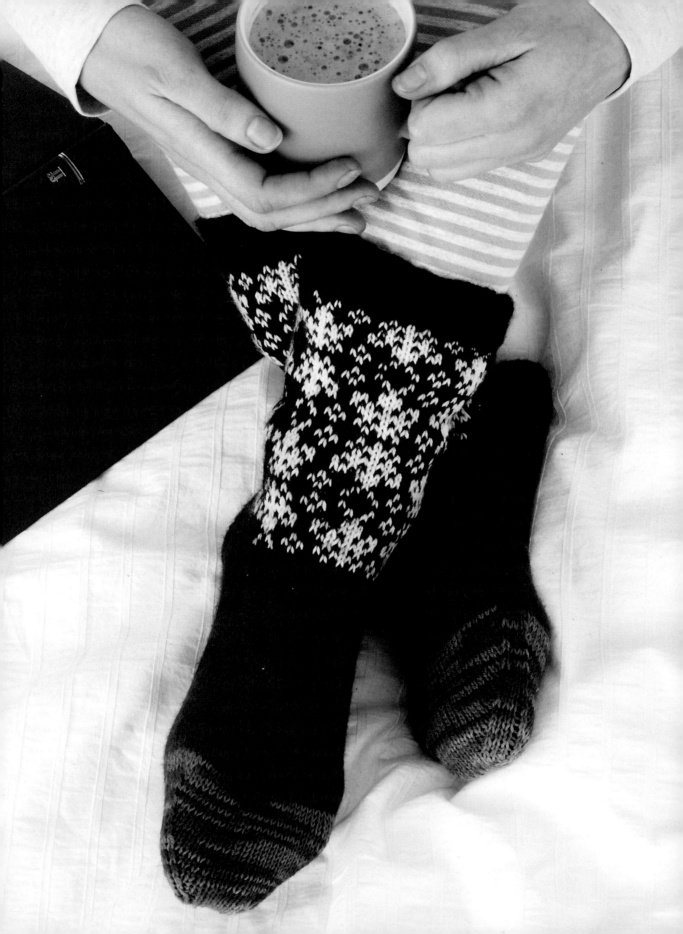

PATTERN NOTES

- For the purposes of this pattern you will need yarn that is packaged as a series of 15 tiny skeins in a set in order to create the gradient effect. Keeping the skeins in this specific order is essential.

- Before you start, number each skein by writing the numbers 1 through 15 on tiny pieces of paper and attaching them to the skeins with pins. The skeins are numbered starting with the lighter end of the spectrum, meaning that the pure white skein should be number 1 and the darkest skein number 15.

- Divide the skeins for knitting the socks. To create two socks that have the desired gradient effect, each of the skeins needs to be divided equally in half.

- Begin with skeins 1–4, carefully dividing each and labeling each half-skein as you go. These four half-skeins will act as the contrast colors on the legs of the socks. The chart will indicate when you should be using which contrast color as you work through it. Set one half of these labeled skeins aside in a safe place for the second sock.

- Divide the yarn for the main color (MC) of the socks, beginning with skein 15 and working backward through skein 8, taking care to label each half-skein and setting one half of each aside for the second sock. The cuff is cast on and worked starting with skein 15. Work until half-skein 15 is used up, leaving a long enough tail to weave in later. Continue with half-skein 14 in the same way, and when it's used up, switch to half-skein 13, and so on.

- Keep in mind that this pattern does not specify when you should switch yarns; simply move on to the next skein when you run out of yarn. The socks as worked in the accompanying images used up skeins 15 down through 8, which are designated as the main color.

Color chart for socks

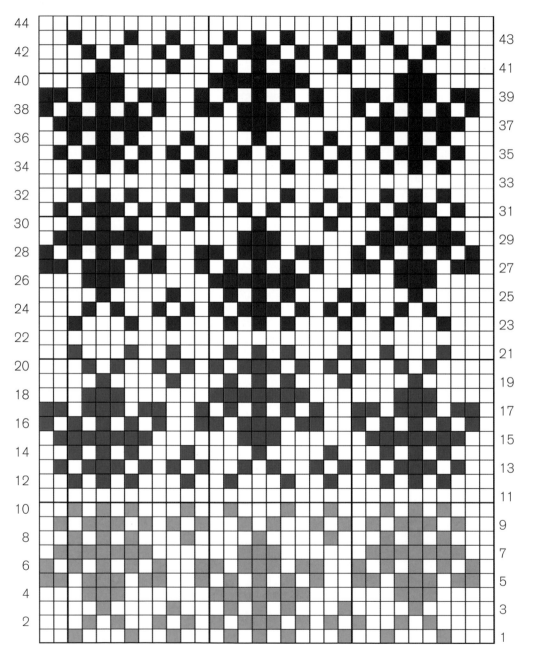

Chart key

☐ MC
◼ CC1
◼ CC2
◼ CC3
◼ CC4

TO MAKE THE SOCKS

CUFF

Using MC, CO 64 sts using Long-Tail CO method (see page 117) or any other stretchy cast-on. Distribute sts evenly across 4 needles with 16 sts on each needle. The needles will now be known as N1, 2, 3, and 4, respectively. Join into round, being careful not to twist sts, pm for beginning of round.

Round 1: [K2 tbl, p2] around.

Rep round 1 for 9 more rounds.

Knit 2 rounds.

WORKING THE LEG

Work rounds 1–44 from chart, reading each round from right to left, and working each chart row twice across each round.

Break C4.

WORKING THE HEEL

The heel is worked back and forth across 32 sts on N1 and N2 with MC only.

Row 1 (RS): With one needle, knit across sts on N1, knit to last st on N2, wrap this st, leave st on RH needle, turn.

Row 2 (WS): Purl to last st, wrap this st, and turn.

Cont as foll:

Row 3: Knit to last 2 sts, w&t.

Row 4: Purl to last 2 sts, w&t.

Row 5: Knit to last 3 sts, w&t.

Row 6: Purl to last 3 sts, w&t.

Cont in this manner, working 1 st less per row until 13 sts are wrapped on either end of heel, ending with a WS row, turn. (6 sts remain in work in middle of heel.)

Row 1 (RS): Knit to first wrapped st, pick up front of wrap and place it on LH ndl, knit wrap and next st tog, w&t (this st is wrapped twice). Note: You may wish to knit the wrap and next st tog tbl to tighten this st.

Row 2 (WS): Purl to first wrapped st, pick up back of wrap and place it on LH ndl, purl wrap and next st tog, w&t (this st is wrapped twice). Note: You may wish to purl the wrap and next st tog tbl to tighten this st.

Row 3: Knit to first double-wrapped st, pick up front of both wraps and place them on LH ndl, knit wraps and next st tog, w&t. Note: You may wish to knit these sts tog tbl to tighten this st.

Row 4: Purl to first double-wrapped st, pick up back of both wraps and place them on LH ndl, purl wraps and next st tog, w&t. Note: You may wish to purl these sts tog tbl to tighten this st.

Repeat rows 3 and 4 until all double-wrapped sts have been worked, ending with a WS row.

Next row (RS): Knit.

WORKING THE FOOT
The foot is worked stockinette st with MC only. Sl half of heel sts to another ndl so that there are 16 sts on each of 4 ndls. Join into rounds again. Rounds begin at center under foot (the first round begins with N2). With N1, pick up 1 st in gap between ndls; N2 and 3, knit, N4, pick up 1 st in gap between N3 and N4, then knit to end. (66 sts)

Next Round:

N1: K8, k2tog, knit to end;

N2: knit;

N3: knit;

N4: k6, ssk, knit to end. (64 sts)

Cont even in stockinette st until piece is approximately 2 in. (5 cm) shorter than desired length. Check to make sure there are 16 sts on each of 4 ndls.

DECREASING FOR THE TOE
Round 1:

N1: Knit to last 3 sts, k2tog, k1;

N2: k1, ssk, knit to end;

N3: knit to last 3 sts, k2tog, k1;

N4: k1, ssk, knit to end. (4 sts dec)

Round 2: Knit.

Rep these 2 rounds 10 more times. (20 sts remain with 5 sts on each ndl)

With N4, knit across sts on N1, sl sts from N3 to N2. (10 sts on each ndl)

Cut yarn, leaving an 18 in. (45.5 cm) long tail to graft remaining sts. Using tail, use kitchener st (see page 122) to join sts at toe.

FINISHING

Weave in all loose ends with a tapestry needle. Block to measurements.

CHAPTER 3
Basic Knitting Techniques

In the following pages, you'll find a guide to the tools, equipment, and core knitting skills that you'll need in order to work the techniques in this book, starting with the essential tools: knitting needles!

Tools and Equipment

Making sure you have the right tools and equipment is essential, whether you are baking a cake or knitting a project. There is more to a successful knit than just needles and yarn. The proper needles and notions will help you on your way to a fantastic finished piece.

NEEDLES

Knitting needles come in a variety of materials, including different types of wood, metal, and plastic. While many knitters have a personal preference as to which material they prefer working with, the proper needles make a difference in the finished result of the work and comfort of the knitter, and will last a lifetime if of high quality.

Needles come in three basic forms: circular, used when knitting in the round for a project like a hat or cowl; straight, used for projects knitted flat, like a scarf; and DPNs, or double-pointed needles, used for small-circumference knitting, such as socks or fingerless mitts.

The size of needle used is dependent upon gauge and yarn weight. Typically sized in both metric and US sizes, needle diameter can be adjusted to help the knitter achieve the desired gauge. The length of the needle is determined by total stitch count. The more stitches a project has, the longer the straight needle—or cord, on a circular needle—needs to be. It is always better to accommodate stitches on a needle smaller than the width or circumference of the finished work, to prevent the stitches from becoming stretched or distorted.

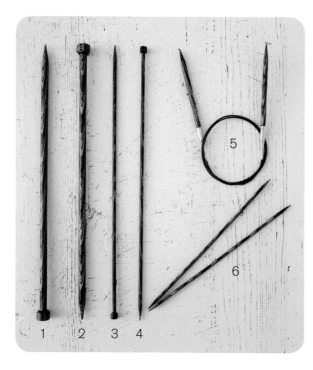

Straight needles (1-4); circular needles (5); double-pointed needles (6)

NOTIONS

Notions are an important factor when working on a project, as well as a fun way to accessorize your hobby. Every knitter jumps at the chance to fill their notions bag with goodies and gadgets designed to make their lives easier and more organized.

TAPE MEASURE

An essential item for your bag, choose a tape measure that shows both inches and centimeters.

NEEDLE GAUGE

Useful for checking or converting needle sizes, and especially useful on old needles where the printed numbers have rubbed off.

ROW COUNTER

You could use a conventional row counter—a small, plastic device that slides neatly onto the end of your needle. Alternatively, many smartphones have apps available to keep track of the number of completed rows, which also allow you to input notes for each pattern.

STITCH MARKERS

Available in a plethora of colors, shapes, and sizes, stitch markers are arguably the notion that knitters use the most. They help you keep track of pattern repeats or the beginning of a round, and are a visual cue to something important happening in the

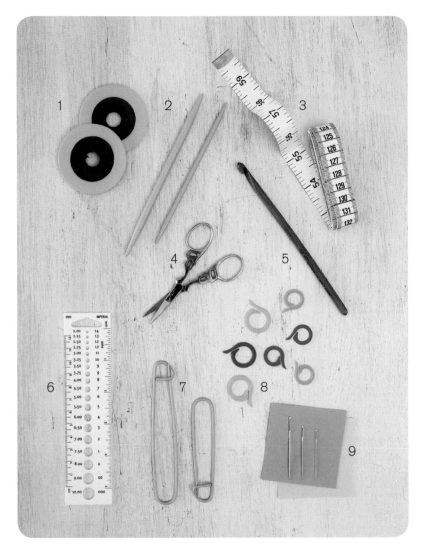

pattern, without affecting gauge or getting in the way.

TAPESTRY NEEDLES

Similar to knitting needles, tapestry or yarn needles come in a variety of materials, with some coming in their own carrying tube. Used primarily for weaving in ends, they can be found in many sizes and with tips of varying bluntness.

Pom-pom maker (1); cable needles (2); tape measure (3); embroidery scissors (4); crochet hook (5); needle gauge (6); stitch holders (7); stitch markers (8); tapestry needles (9)

CROCHET HOOK

Every good knitter should know how to wield a crochet hook. Used for certain cast-on methods, crochet hooks come in as many sizes as knitting needles do, and are a very helpful tool for rescuing dropped stitches and making fringe.

DESIGN TOOLS

Keeping your place in a pattern, or even designing your own chart or schematic, is not always easy. A bright highlighter, sticky notes for keeping track of a row in a chart, knitting graph paper for designing, and colored pencils make this process a smooth, organized one.

SCISSORS

A sharp pair of embroidery scissors that comes in its own sheath is essential.

BUTTON STASH

As if knitters needed an excuse to buy buttons! Having a button stash is just as essential as having an eclectic yarn stash. Many patterns call for buttons, and with countless materials, shapes, sizes, and colors available, it's worth building up your button stash right away.

STITCH HOLDERS

Often used to put a section of knitting in "time out," stitch holders come in many lengths and are made of metal or plastic. Keep a few different sizes in your notions bag to accommodate any length of stitches.

WASTE YARN

Keeping a small stash of waste yarn on hand is helpful because it can act as a stand-in for a stitch marker, be used to keep stitches live when knitting needles need to be borrowed for another project, or be used when a cast-on or other technique calls for it. By keeping a bit of each yarn weight on hand, the knitter will always be sure to have the equivalent weight (or thinner) to the working yarn so stitches do not get stretched. Dental floss works well in a pinch.

CABLE NEEDLE

When choosing a cable needle, it is important to keep the size as close to the size of the knitting needle as possible. Often coming in sets of three, cable needles come in wood, plastic, and metal in a variety of shapes and lengths.

POM-POM MAKER

Some knitters prefer to make their pom-poms with hand-cut circles of card (see page 25); however, pom-pom makers can be a useful expedient. They often come in multipacks to allow for different sizes, and some are fancier than others, but all result in the perfect pom-pom.

BLOCKING TOOLS

Talk to any knitter about blocking and you'll get an earful! While everyone has their own method, having proper tools—like a blocking mat with 1 in. (2.5 cm) squares to allow for fast and easy measuring, T-pins, wires for large geometric projects, a spray bottle, iron, steamer, wooden sock and mittens blockers, and a head form—allows the knitter to take their project from good to great, giving it a finished, polished look.

Choosing Yarn

Choosing the ideal yarn can make or break a project. Stitches react differently when worked in different fibers; color is a big factor; allergies to certain fibers are a consideration; the cost of fiber may sway your choice; and availability is, of course, a factor.

Knowing what is in your yarn is as important as knowing what is in the food you consume. This knowledge is especially crucial if fiber allergies or animal ethics are a concern. Luckily, knitters today are spoiled for choice by the wide variety of protein, cellulose, synthetic, and fiber blends available at local yarn shops and fiber festivals.

ANIMAL FIBERS

Some of the warmest yarns available are made from protein, or animal, fibers. They are widely used and preferred by many knitters. Animal fibers have scales on the shaft of the fiber, and it is these scales that mean animal fibers and blends can be "felted"—a process whereby the yarn is shrunk down with heat, water, and friction. Because of the the scales on the shaft of the fiber, different grades and qualities of animal fibers are available. For example, if the scales have been removed as part of a chemical process, the yarn is referred to as "superwash" and can be cleaned without the risk of felting. The scales also trap air, making animal knits extra warm and the first choice for many in cold-weather climates.

Natural animal fiber options: Angora, cashgora, camel, cashmere, llama, mohair, opossum, pashmina, qiviut, silk, wool, yak.

PLANT FIBERS

An excellent choice for those living in warmer areas, or for knitters with fiber allergies or animal ethics concerns, cellulose or plant fibers are available in a veritable smorgasbord of options. Because the shaft of plant fibers is largely porous, the air and negative space make these fibers lightweight and breathable.

Natural cellulose fiber options: Bamboo, cotton, flax/linen, hemp.

SYNTHETIC FIBERS

Sometimes the best choice is to use synthetic fiber. Introduced to the textile world in the mid-1930s, these yarns are inexpensive to make, resist potential issues such as moths or mildew, and are washable, making them a common go-to for baby and large-scale knitting.

Synthetic fiber options: Acrylic, microfiber, nylon, polyester.

Cellulosic fiber options: Rayon.

SUBSTITUTING YARNS

You may find yourself substituting the yarn called for in a pattern to meet your own individual needs. The most important goal in yarn subbing is to match gauge. While each yarn band has a recommended gauge listed, the most accurate way to see if the yarn is an even swap is to knit a swatch in the chosen pattern (see page 115). It is also necessary to think about how different fibers react to different stitches and techniques. Plant fibers tend to grow when wet blocked while synthetics may have little give. Animal fibers are a better option for stranded colorwork because of the scales on the fiber, but a superwash makes for a longer-lasting knitted sock. The only answer is to swatch, swatch, swatch!

HOW TO READ A YARN BAND

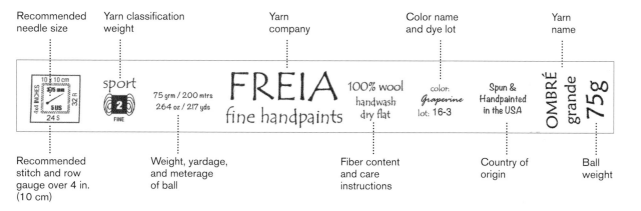

Recommended needle size

Yarn classification weight

Yarn company

Color name and dye lot

Yarn name

FREIA
fine handpaints

100% wool
handwash
dry flat

color:
Grapevine
lot: 16-3

Spun &
Handpainted
in the USA

OMBRÉ grande 75g

sport
2
FINE

75 grm / 200 mtrs
2.64 oz / 217 yds

Recommended stitch and row gauge over 4 in. (10 cm)

Weight, yardage, and meterage of ball

Fiber content and care instructions

Country of origin

Ball weight

CATEGORIES OF YARN

Yarn	Lace including Fingering 10-count crochet thread	Super Fine including Fingering, Sock, and Baby	Fine including Sport and Baby	Light including DK and Light Worsted	Medium including Worsted, Aran, and Afghan	Bulky including Chunky, Craft, and Rug	Super Bulky including Super Bulky and Roving	Jumbo including Jumbo and Roving
	0	1	2	3	4	5	6	7
Knit gauge range in stockinette stitch to 4 in. (10 cm)	33–40 sts	27–32 sts	23–26 sts	21–24 sts	16–20 sts	12–15 sts	7–11 sts	6 sts and fewer
Recommended needle in metric size range	1.5–2.25 mm	2.25–3.25 mm	3.25–3.75 mm	3.75–4.5 mm	4.5–5.5 mm	5.5–8 mm	8–12.75 mm	12.75 mm and larger
Recommended needle US size range	000–1	1–3	3–5	5–7	7–9	9–11	11–17	17 and larger

Getting Started

HOLDING THE YARN

There are dozens of ways to hold yarn when knitting. If you're a Continental or European knitter, the yarn is held in the left hand and "picked," but American and English knitters hold the yarn in the right hand and "throw."

No matter what type of knitter you are, or which hand you hold the yarn in, a source of tension must be established so as to control the yarn and create an even gauge in the stitches. While there is no wrong way to hold the yarn, it's best to try different options until one feels right, especially if you have joint or wrist issues.

CONTINENTAL METHOD
Continental knitters often find it comfortable to wrap the yarn around the pinkie, then drape it over the index finger on the left hand, creating two sources of tension.

ENGLISH METHOD
English-style knitters weave the yarn over their ring finger, under the middle finger, and then back over the index finger.

MEASURING GAUGE

Measuring gauge and working to a certain gauge are essential for knitting. Because each knitter may have different natural tension, it is imperative to swatch and measure gauge before casting on for any project.

Gauge is the amount of stitches per inch (2.5 cm) in a piece of knitted fabric running horizontally and the amount of rows or rounds per inch (2.5 cm) running vertically up the work.

Gauge is generally measured in a 4 x 4 in. (10 x 10 cm) square. A swatch is made in the correct pattern using the needles and yarn suggested for the finished project to ensure it matches the ideal gauge for the pattern. A gauge swatch should actually be made to a minimum size of 6 x 6 in. (15 x 15 cm) to get an accurate reading without worrying about edges that may curl in and distort the measurement.

Having too many stitches or rows in the gauge-measuring area results in a project that will be too small, whereas having too few means the project will be too large. By adjusting needle size, the pattern gauge can be achieved, resulting in a perfectly fitting garment.

Many patterns call for a "blocked gauge." Blocking is a process of using either water or steam to even out your stitches, and relax the yarn, allowing you to adjust sizing (see page 134). The gauge swatch should be blocked according to the method with which the finished project will be blocked before being evaluated.

READING CHARTS

Charts are a visual representation of a written pattern. Not only do charts offer a preview of the finished design, they can also be easier and more intuitive to follow than line after line of text. Most charts are a slice of a repeating pattern, delineated by a bold line. The pattern will say how many repeats are needed.

Each stitch is characterized by a unique symbol in a single square representing one stitch, followed by an explanation for execution. As you would when reading a map, it's important to look over the key or legend before getting started, as charts can vary in their use of symbol definitions.

Charts worked in the round are always read from right to left, bottom to top, in the same direction as the knitting is worked. If the piece is being worked in rows, right side rows will be worked from right to left, and wrong side rows will be worked from left to right and from bottom to top. Charts do not always have the wrong sides charted out if they represent resting rows that are simply purled or knit across.

CASTING ON

There are dozens of different techniques for casting on. Different methods are used to give different results; for example, a tighter edging, a stretchy edging, or a decorative edging. While many beginners use only one basic method for everything, it's good to have some options in your knitting repertoire. As your skills increase, you'll be able to decide which is the best option depending on the type of project you're knitting. In the following pages, you'll find instructions for the various cast-on methods used in this book.

KNITTED CAST-ON

This cast-on is slower than some alternatives and is worked with two needles, but it is easy to remember how to execute—a good choice for a project that needs a sturdy, somewhat stretchy edging.

1 Begin by making a slipknot, leaving a 6–8 in. (15–20 cm) tail. Place the slipknot onto a needle. This will be the left-hand needle.

2 Insert the right-hand needle into the stitch as if to knit it.

3 Knit the stitch, but do not pull the stitch off the left-hand needle.

4 Twist and transfer the incomplete stitch from the right-hand needle to the left-hand needle.

5 Begin the sequence again, working off the stitch on the left-hand needle closest to the tip.

6 Each repetition adds another stitch to the left-hand needle until the desired number of stitches is reached.

LONG-TAIL CAST-ON

This is often the method that beginners learn first. Stretchy yet firm, the edge counts as the first knitted row and pairs nicely with garter, ribbing, or stockinette.

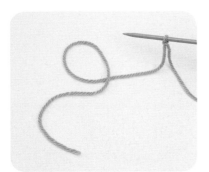

1. Make a slipknot, leaving a tail long enough for the number of stitches you need to cast on. Place the slipknot on a needle; this will be the right-hand needle.

2. Part the yarn using your thumb and index finger, and pull the needle down to make a slingshot. The working yarn should come from the bottom.

3. Bring the needle through the loop on the thumb from the bottom up.

4. Bring the needle over and through the loop on the index finger, grabbing the yarn.

5. Then, pull the needle through the loop on the thumb.

6. Let the loop on the thumb slip off, and snug up the stitch.

PROVISIONAL CAST-ON

Sometimes called "The Temporary Cast-On," this is a classic cast-on for a project that will have ends joined later, have additional work added on, or be turned in to create a knitted hem.

  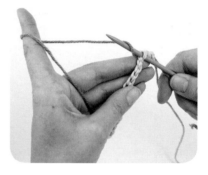

1 With crochet hook and single-ply, contrasting-color waste yarn, begin by making a slipknot and placing the slipknot on the hook.

2 Chain the required number of cast-on stitches, plus a few extra. Cut the yarn, pulling the end through to secure the chain.

3 With the right-hand needle, insert the tip into the raised bump on the back of the chain as if to knit. Introduce the working yarn, leaving a 6–8 in. (15–20 cm) tail, and fully execute the knit stitch into the picked-up bump from the chain.

4 There will now be a complete stitch on the right-hand needle.

5 Repeat this process until the number of cast-on stitches required is on the right-hand needle. Leave the waste yarn in place, to be removed at the end.

GERMAN TWISTED CAST-ON

Often referred to as "The Old Norwegian Cast-On," this variation of the long-tail method provides more give. A tidy and stretchy edge makes this the perfect cast-on for hats and socks.

1 Begin by making a slipknot, leaving a tail
... long enough to accommodate the number of stitches you need to cast on. The yarn can be wrapped around the needle the same number of times as there are cast-on stitches for the estimated length needed. Place the slipknot on a needle; this will be the right-hand needle.

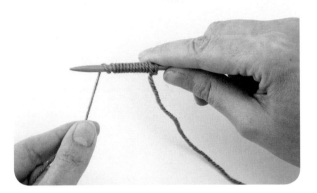

2 Using the thumb and index
... finger on your left hand, part the yarn. Holding the needle in the right hand, pull the needle down, making a slingshot. The working yarn should be coming from the bottom.

3 Bring the needle under
... both strands of the loop on the thumb.

4 Bring the needle from the
... top down through the loop on the thumb.

(Continued on next page.)

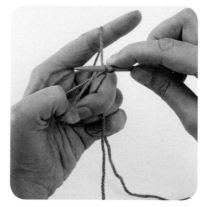

5... Bring the needle over and through the loop on the index finger, grabbing the yarn.

6... Point the thumb downward, letting the loop untwist and open up. Do not let the loop fall off the thumb.

7... Pull the needle through, letting the loop slip off, and snug up the stitch.

CABLE CAST-ON

Superb for projects that require a firm edging, such as the bottom of a cardigan, this method is similar to the knitted cast-on and is worked with two needles, providing a sturdy, non-stretchy edge.

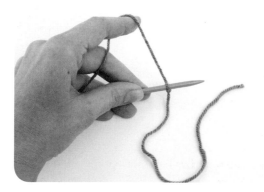

1... Begin by making a slipknot, leaving a 6–8 in. (15–20 cm) tail. Place the slipknot onto a needle. This will be the left-hand needle.

2... Cast one stitch onto the left-hand needle using the knitted cast-on method (see page 116). There will now be two stitches.

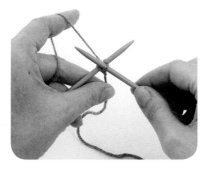  

3 Insert the right-hand needle between the two stitches. Knit into this space, leaving both stitches in place on the left-hand needle.

4 Twist and transfer the incomplete stitch from the right-hand needle to the left-hand needle.

5 Tighten up the stitch. You will now have three stitches on the left-hand needle.

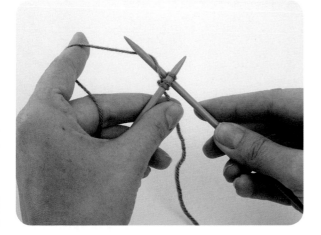 

6 Begin the sequence again, always working between the two stitches on the left-hand needle closest to the tip.

7 Each repeat of the process adds another stitch to the left-hand needle until the desired number of stitches is reached.

Kitchener Stitch

Kitchener stitch, sometimes called "grafting" or "weaving," is used to join two sets of stitches of equal amounts that are still live on the needles. Using a tapestry needle threaded with yarn to make an additional row that looks like knit stitches between them, a seamless join is created that, when done correctly, is impossible to see. This technique can be a little tricky to master at first, but is great for closing up the toes of socks and joining shoulders and hoods.

1 Start by dividing the total number of stitches equally over two needles and hold needles parallel with wrong sides of work facing.

2 Work the set-up by inserting a threaded tapestry needle into the first stitch on the front needle purlwise and pull through, leaving the stitch on the needle.

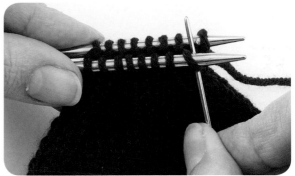

3 Insert the tapestry needle into the first stitch on the back needle knitwise and pull through, leaving the stitch on the needle. Steps 2 and 3 are worked only once.

4 Begin sequence by inserting the tapestry needle into the first stitch on the front needle knitwise and pull through, letting the stitch drop off the needle.

5 Insert the tapestry needle into the second stitch on the front needle purlwise, leaving the stitch on the needle.

6 Insert the tapestry needle into the first stitch on the back needle purlwise and pull through, letting the stitch drop off the needle.

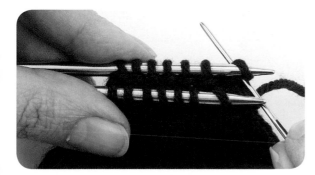

7 Insert the tapestry needle into the second stitch on the back needle knitwise, leaving the stitch on the needle.

8 Repeat Steps 4–7 until all stitches are worked, tightening up as needed.

Shaping

Certain projects require knitters to manipulate the shape of the knitted fabric while it is still being worked on the needles. To achieve shaping for waistlines, necklines, the tops of hats, mittens, shawls, and toys, stitches can be added or removed. There are many different methods of adding or taking away stitches—your pattern should usually tell you which method is preferred.

INCREASE METHODS

KNIT THROUGH THE FRONT AND BACK (KFB)

1 ... Work to the stitch that is to be increased. Knit into the stitch but do not slip the stitch off the left-hand needle.

2 ... Throw the needle around and to the back of the stitch, and knit through the back loop. Pull the stitch off the needle.

3 ... The finished sequence creates an extra stitch on the right-hand needle.

MAKE 1 RIGHT (M1R)

1... Work to where the increase should be made and pull the work apart slightly to see the horizontal thread running between the stitches.

2... With the left-hand needle, pick up the running thread and take it from the back to the front.

3... With the right-hand needle, knit into the front of this lifted stitch, then slide it off the left-hand needle.

MAKE 1 LEFT (M1L)

4... The finished sequence creates a right-leaning increase on the right-hand needle.

1... Work to where the increase should be made and pull the work apart slightly to see the horizontal thread running between the stitches. With the right-hand needle, pick up the running thread and take it from the back to the front.

2... Use the left-hand needle to go through the front of the stitch, and knit into the back with the right-hand needle and then slide it off the left-hand needle. The finished sequence creates a left-leaning increase on the right-hand needle.

YARN OVER (YO)

1 Bring the yarn to the front of the work, then continue in pattern. This creates an open increase.

DECREASE METHODS

KNIT 2 TOGETHER (K2TOG)

1 Work to the two stitches to be decreased. Insert the right-hand needle into the far-left stitch and then the near-left stitch and knit them together.

2 The finished sequence creates a right-leaning stitch on the right-hand needle.

SLIP SLIP KNIT (SSK)

1 Work to where you need to make the decrease. Slip the first stitch on the left-hand needle as if to knit to the right-hand needle.

2 Slip the next stitch on the left-hand needle as if to knit to the right-hand needle.

3 Insert the left-hand needle into the front of the two slipped stitches on the right-hand needle.

4 Knit those two stitches together.

5 The finished sequence creates a left-leaning stitch on the right-hand needle.

Circular Knitting

When working on a project that is circular, such as a hat, pair of gloves or socks, or a cowl, knitting in the round is an obvious choice. For these items, circular knitting results in much faster knitting, with a more even gauge, and the finished item fits better than if the work were knit flat and seamed.

USING CIRCULAR NEEDLES

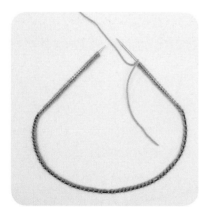

1 Using the method of your choice, cast on the required number of stitches. They should fill the entire needle comfortably. If the stitches are crowded, change to a larger circular needle. If there are not enough stitches to go around, change to a smaller circular needle.

2 Making sure all the stitches are facing the same way without any twisting, join into the round by knitting the first stitch.

3 Place a stitch marker to delineate the beginning of the round and continue working in pattern.

USING DOUBLE-POINTED NEEDLES

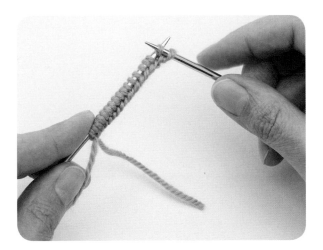

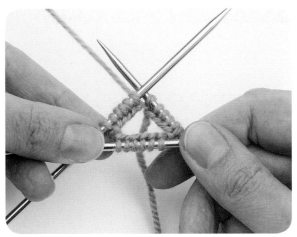

1. Using a method of your choice, cast the required number of stitches onto one double-pointed needle. Distribute the stitches evenly onto three or four DPNs, as specified in the pattern.

2. Join the work into a triangle or square, depending on the number of DPNs being used. Make sure all the stitches are facing the same way without any twisting.

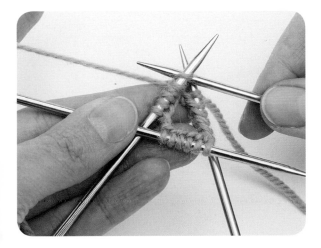

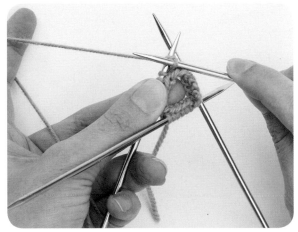

3. Introduce the fourth (or fifth) needle by knitting into the first stitch at the beginning of the round. This is the working needle.

4. When all the stitches on the left-hand needle have been worked, the right-hand needle will be full and the empty needle will become the working needle.

Finishing

BINDING OFF

Binding off is how live stitches at the end of a project are passed over each other, essentially locking them down so they cannot unravel. Patterns usually dictate which binding-off method to use, and while there are many different ways to secure an edge, the most common are knit bind-off and purl bind-off.

The knit bind-off and purl bind-off techniques that follow are typically used for finishing off stockinette stitch; a combination of the two techniques is reserved for stitches such as ribbing.

BASIC KNIT BIND-OFF

1 Knit the first two stitches. With the left-hand needle, pick up the first stitch on the right-hand needle and pull it up and over the second stitch, allowing it to fall off.

2 One stitch remains. Continue this sequence, always working two stitches at a time. A braided edge will take shape off the right-hand needle.

PURL BIND-OFF

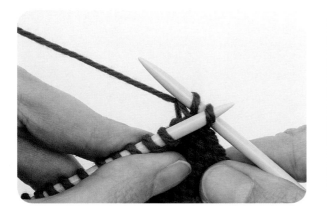 

1... Purl the first two stitches. With the left-hand needle, pick up the first stitch on the right-hand needle and pull it up and over the second stitch, allowing it to fall off.

2... One stitch remains. Continue this sequence, always working two stitches at a time. A stretchy braided edge will take shape off the right-hand needle.

BIND-OFF IN RIB

1... Knit the knit stitch and purl the purl stitch for the first two stitches. With the left-hand needle, pick up the first stitch on the right-hand needle and pull it up and over the second stitch, allowing it to fall off.

2... One stitch remains. Continue this sequence, always working two stitches at a time. A braided edge will take shape off the right-hand needle.

WEAVING IN ENDS

Weaving in ends is a very important part of finishing the work. All ends should be woven in for at least 3 in. (8 cm), no matter which method is chosen. That way, if the ends begin to pop out, they will be long enough to unpick back to the source, be put on a tapestry needle, and be woven back in.

GARTER STITCH

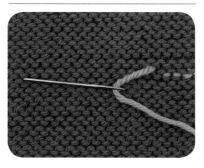

Garter stitch is made up of "smile shapes" and "frown shapes." Thread the tapestry needle onto the yarn tail and work into your chosen stitch, weaving the needle into each stitch, from the bottom up, for 3 in. (8 cm) across.

RIBBING

Thread the tapestry needle and, working in one half of the "V"-shaped knit stitch, weave the needle into each half of stitch, from the bottom up, for 3 in. (8 cm) vertically.

TROUBLESHOOTING

Mistakes happen, and sometimes a few stitches or even a few rows or rounds need to be taken back. When taking back individual stitches, it is referred to as to "tink," which is "knit" spelled backwards. "Frogging" is similar to the sound a frog makes, when the knitter has to "rip it, rip it." It's a good idea to get used to doing both, because if you can fix your own mistakes, it only makes you a better knitter.

TINKING

Using the left-hand needle, put the tip into the stitch below the right-hand needle. Push it through from front to back and let the yarn pop out, unknitting the stitch.

FROGGING

To pull out more than a few stitches, remove the knitting needles from the work and lay flat on a table. Gently unravel the yarn to the desired spot.

JOINING YARN

There are quite a few ways to join yarn into a project, whether the knitter has run out or the yarn has been broken. Personally, I dislike having yarn waste, so I do not wait until the end of the row or round to join in a new skein. I like to join it in when it runs out.

SPLICING YARN

1. Begin by slightly unplying the end of the old yarn and the beginning of the new yarn.

2. Overlap the unplied ends and add in a bit of water.

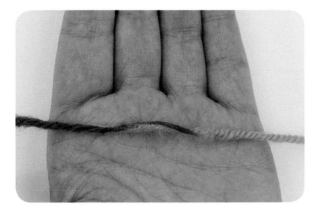

3. Rub your hands together to hand-felt the ends together. Felting works by applying heat, water, and friction.

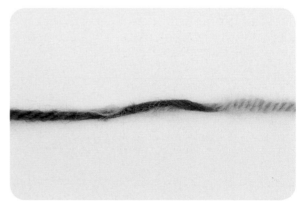

4. Once the yarn is dry, it is ready to be knit.

BLOCKING

Blocking takes a project from good to great. Not only can blocking even out stitches and make the work look more polished and finished, but for certain techniques, such as lace, it will open up the work and let the beauty shine through. Steam blocking is a technique generally used for finishing a project without changing the size. Wet blocking is a way to finish a project and make it grow larger.

STEAM BLOCKING

WET BLOCKING

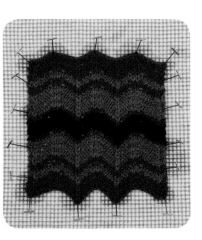

1 Begin by pinning the work
... to size on a suitable surface (one that can get wet). Spray the work all over with a spray bottle until it is damp to the touch.

2 With a handheld steamer, or
... using an iron with a steam setting, blast the work all over with steam, hovering 1 in. (2.5 cm) above the work and taking care to keep your face and hands away from the steam. Do not place the iron or steamer directly on the work. Allow the work to dry completely before unpinning.

Begin by submerging the work in cold water with a wool wash for 15 minutes. Knead the excess water out of the work (do not wring) and lay flat on a towel. Roll up the towel and stand on it, squeezing out all extra water. Pin the work into shape on a suitable surface (one that can get wet). Allow the work to dry completely before unpinning.

About the Designers

AUTHOR: TANIS GRAY

Blocket Hat; Stripey Blanket; Thrummed Mittens

A graduate of the Rhode Island School of Design, Tanis lives in Fairfax, VA, with her green mechanical engineer husband, son, and daughter. Having worked at Martha Stewart, HBO, Focus Features, in the art department in the film and television industries, and as the yarn editor at *Vogue Knitting* and co-editor of *Knit.1*, she has many years of experience working in the creative field.

Tanis has over 450 published knitting designs, and her work has been featured in many major publications and books worldwide, including on twelve covers. Check out her award-winning books *Knit Local: Celebrating America's Homegrown Yarns; Capitol Knits; Knitting Architecture; Cozy Knits; From Mama, with Love; 3 Skeins or Less—Fresh Knitted Accessories; Wanderlust—46 Modern Knits for Bohemian Style;* and *Modern Baby Knits.*

Tanis is a proud member of the Martha Washington Chapter of the Daughters of the American Revolution (DAR) and the Washington, DC, Chapter of the Mayflower Society. Follow her on Ravelry as TanisKnits and subscribe to her blog at *tanisknits.com.*

Stripey Blanket, see page 37

KIRSTEN KAPUR

Zigzag Legwarmers

New York City-based designer Kirsten has been knitting, sewing, and crafting for as long as she can remember. She worked in ready-to-wear for many years as both an apparel and a textile designer. During those years, she gained a strong knowledge of garment construction as well as of surface design. Kirsten loves designing knitwear because it allows her to combine her construction skills with her sense of color and texture. Kirsten's independently published designs can be found online on Ravelry and her website *kirstenkapurdesigns.com*. Her most recent book is *Drop Dead Easy Knits,* which she co-authored with Gale Zucker and Mary Lou Egan.

Gradient Block Cowl, see page 51

HANNA MACIEJEWSKA

Gradient Block Cowl

Hanna's grandmother taught her how to knit when she was a little girl. She knitted sweaters all the time in school—all her own creations—but only a few years ago realized that knitting and designing knitwear is truly her biggest passion. Since there are countless new ideas in her head at any given time, she prefers to construct her garments and accessories as smartly and seamlessly as possible to save time on finishing and move on to the next idea. Nature and time spent in her garden provide Hanna with an abundance of inspiration, giving her impressions and memories to draw upon later. Hanna is also the proud mother of a beautiful girl, who sometimes draws things for her to knit. Find Hanna at *hadaknits.com* or on Ravelry as hada131.

CARINA SPENCER

Color-Study Cowl

Carina is a wife, mother, and seeker of beauty and truth, and has an undefended passion for the process of creation. Carina lives in Kansas City, MO, with her husband and two girls. She is professionally trained and continues to work as a natural foods personal chef, but found her true passion in knitting design when pregnant with her second child. She immediately recognized that all the elements that drew her to culinary arts were there in the yarn and needles. As a designer, Carina's goal is to create simply constructed, stylish garments and accessories with unique elements that are fun to knit and easy to wear. Read more about Carina at *carinaspencer.com*.

JANE DUPUIS

Festoon Mittens; Moth Socks

SpillyJane (a.k.a. Jane Dupuis) is the author of *SpillyJane Knits Mittens* (Cooperative Press, 2015). Keep up with what she gets up to and into at *spillyjane.blogspot.com*. Jane lives in Windsor, Ontario, in a 100-year-old house with her husband and their buddy, Earl the African Grey Parrot.

ANN WEAVER

Modular Scarf

Ann sees knitting patterns in container ships, Tom Waits lyrics, *Moby-Dick*, classic cocktails, and the work of artists such as Josef Albers and Mark Rothko. She has been designing knitwear since 2007. When she is not traveling to teach knitting workshops, Ann lives in Baltimore, where she works as a freelance editor and writer, and spends her free time volunteering and working to bring change to her community. You can follow Ann on Instagram and find her designs on Ravelry as weaverknits.

MINDY WILKES

Lacy Stripe Shawl

Mindy lives in suburban Cincinnati, Ohio, with her husband, two children, and entirely too much yarn and tea. Mindy loves to design accessories, especially ones that feature lace. Her designs can be found in *Interweave Knits, Knitscene, Pom Pom Quarterly,* and other publications. She can be found online at *mindywilkesdesigns.com* and on Ravelry as Mindy.

Festoon Mittens, see page 60

Yarns Used
in the Projects

Lesson 1:
Knits & Purls, Blocket Hat
Schoppel Wolle/Skacel Collection Gradient: 100% Virgin Merino Wool, 284 yd. (260 m) per 3.5 oz. (100 g). 1 ball in Blues #2198.

Lesson 2:
Slip-Stitch, Color-Study Cowl
Copper Corgi Sport-Weight Gradient Mini-Skein Set: 100% Superwash Merino Wool, 360 yd. (329 m) in six 60 yd. (55 m) skeins. 1 set in Wine Rose Grape.

Lesson 3:
Alternating Stripes, Stripey Blanket
Twisted Fiber Arts Queen: 100% Superwash Merino, 130 yd. (119 m) per 2.5 oz. (70 g). 3 balls in Quip (teal gradient, A) and 2 balls in Magic Hour (orange gradient, B).

Lesson 4:
Thrumming, Thrummed Mittens
Cascade Yarns Melilla: 45% Silk, 35% Merino Wool, 20% Nylon, 220 yd. (200 m) per 3.5 oz. (100 g). 1 skein in #09 Greys.

Neighborhood Fiber Co. Empire Roving: 100% Falkland Wool, 4 oz. (113 g). 1 braid in Fete.

Lesson 5:
Cabling, Gradient Block Cowl
Neighborhood Fiber Co. Studio Chunky: 100% Merino Superwash, 275 yd. (251 m) per 8 oz. (227 g). 1 skein in Charles Centre (MC1) and 1 skein in Thomas Circle (MC2).

Neighborhood Fiber Co. Studio Chunky Gradients: 100% Merino Superwash, 360 yd. (329 m) per 10 oz. (300 g). 1 set of 5 mini-skeins, 72 yd. (66 m) per 2 oz. (60 g) each (CC1, CC2, CC3, CC4, and CC5) in Shades of Jade (CC1–5).

Lesson 6:
Fair Isle, Festoon Mittens
SweetGeorgia Tough Love Sock: 80% Superwash Merino, 20% nylon, 425 yd. (389 m) per 4 oz. (113 g) skein. 1 skein in Nightshade (MC).

Party of Five Tough Love Sock Mini-Skeins: 80% Superwash Merino, 20% nylon; 105 yd. (96 m) per 1 oz. (28 g) skein. 1 set of 5 mini-skeins in Snapdragon. [CC1] Lettuce Wrap, [CC2] Pistachio, [CC3] Melon, [CC4] Birch, [CC5] Orchid.

Lesson 7:
Intarsia, Zigzag Legwarmers
Freia Fine Hand Paints Ombré Sport: 100% Single Ply Wool, 217 yd. (200 m) per 2.64 oz. (75 g). 2 balls in Grapevine.

Lesson 8:
Lace, Lacy Stripe Shawl
Miss Babs Yummy 2-Ply Toes: 100% Superwash Merino Wool, 798 yd. (730 m) per 7.5 oz. (213 g) in Sunflowers. 1 set of 6 mini-skeins, 133 yd. (122 m) per 1.3 oz. (37 g) each.

Lesson 9:
Modular Knitting, Modular Scarf
Dragonfly Fibers Traveller Gradient Set: 100% Superwash Merino; 140 yd. (128 m) per 2 oz. (57 g) skein. 1 kit containing 6 skeins in Bad Moon Rising.

Lesson 10:
Wrap & Turn Short Rows, Moth Socks
Fiber Optic Yarns Foot Notes Paintbox Gradient: 80% Superwash Merino Wool, 20% nylon, 450 yd. (411 m) per 4.3 oz. (122 g) skein. 1 set in Raspberry to Cream.

Abbreviations

2/2 LC	slip 2 stitches to cable needle and hold in front, k2, k2 from cable needle
2/2 RC	slip 2 stitches to cable needle and hold in back, k2, k2 from cable needle
C	color
CC	contrasting color
CO	cast on
Cont	continue
dec	decrease/d
DPN	double-pointed needle(s)
foll	following/s
inc	increase/d
k	knit
LH	left-hand
k1 tbl	knit 1 stitch through back loop
k2tog	knit 2 stitches together
k2tog-tbl	knit 2 stitches together through back loops
kfb	knit into the front and back of the next st
M1L	From the back, lift the horizontal strand between stitches with the left needle and knit through the front loop.
M1R	From the front, lift the horizontal strand between stitches with the left needle and knit through the back loop.

ndl	needle
p	purl
p2tog	purl 2 stitches together as one stitch
patt	pattern
pm	place marker
rep	repeat
RH	right-hand
RS	right side
s2kp	Slip 2 sts as if to k2tog, k1, pass slipped sts over—2 sts decreased.
sk2p	Slip 1 st as if to knit, k2tog, pass slipped st over—2 sts decreased.
sl	slip st as if to purl
sm	slip marker
ssk	slip, slip, knit slipped sts together
st(s)	stitch(es)
tbl	through the back leg of loop
w&t	wrap and turn
WS	wrong side
wyib	with yarn in back
wyif	with yarn in front
yo	yarn over

Index

Acknowledgments

Dedication: For Beth Gensheimer Newman, the best teacher I know.

My deepest gratitude to the talented and brilliant designers who accepted the challenge of gradient knitwear design—Ann Weaver, Carina Spencer, Hanna Maciejewska, Jane Dupuis, Kirsten Kapur, and Mindy Wilkes. You are a classy bunch of knitters, and I am honored to be in your company.

For bringing the projects to life, thanks to photographer Simon Pask and the lovely models Virginia Lee of Spotlight and Grace St. Hill at PARTS agency.

Many thanks to amazing photographer Brandy Crist-Travers and proficient hand model Jessica Dekker for demonstrating the step-by-step techniques.

Special thanks to Emma Harverson and Julia Shone for your constant guidance and grace.

For the generous supply of fiber, gratitude to:

Cascade Yarns
cascadeyarns.com

The Copper Corgi Fiber Studio
Savannah, GA
thecoppercorgi.com

Dragonfly Fibers
4104 Howard Avenue
Kensington, MD 20895
301.312.6883
dragonflyfibers.com

Fiber Optic Yarns
726 Mohawk Trail
Milford, OH 45150
513.248.0752
kimberbaldwindesigns.com

Freia Fine Handpaints
6023 Christie Avenue
Emeryville, CA 94608
1.800.595.KNIT (5648)
freiafibers.com

Miss Babs Hand-Dyed Yarns & Fibers
P.O. Box 78
Mountain City, TN 37683
423.727.0670
missbabs.com

Neighborhood Fiber Co
700 N. Eutaw Street
Baltimore, MD 21201
410.989.3770
neighborhoodfiberco.com

Schoppel Wolle/Skacel Collection
P.O. Box 88110
Seattle, WA 98138-2110
800.255.1278
skacelknitting.com

SweetGeorgia
110-408 East Kent Avenue
Vancouver BC, V5X 2X7 Canada
604.569.6811
sweetgeorgiayarns.com

Twisted Fiber Arts
202 S. Park Street
P.O. Box 721
Mason, MI 48854
517-833-9144
twistedfiberart.com

Loop London
15 Camden Passage
London
N1 8EA
www.loopknitting.com
Instagram: looplondonloves

High praise to Ann Barrett, Therese Chynoweth, Katie Crous, Lindsay Kaubi, Jodi Lewanda, Michelle Pickering, and Luise Roberts for their editorial work and technical expertise.

Quantum Books would like to thank the following for supplying images for inclusion in this book: Shutterstock.com, Albachiaraa, page 12.